# FISHING LURES: A PRACTICAL GUIDE

BY THE SAME AUTHOR
*Fishing Flies and their Plumage*

# FISHING LURES

## A Practical Guide

# MICHAEL VEALE

° THE °
SPORTSMAN'S
PRESS
*LONDON*

Published by The Sportsman's Press 1992

© S. M. Veale 1992

A catalogue record for this book
is available from the British Library

ISBN–0–948253–58–4

Printed in Great Britain by
Redwood Press Limited, Melksham, Wiltshire

# Contents

*Acknowledgements*                                                    viii

*List of Plates*                                                       vii

*Introduction*                                                          1

1   Spinners and hooks                                                  3
    *Different types of spinners and hooks, their construction and
    how hooks are made. Tools needed to construct your own
    spinners and how to do it.*

2   Fishing the Spinning Lure                                          10
    *Early tackle and its uses. Spinning techniques. Correct lures for
    the prevailing fishing conditions. General waterside advice, boat
    safety and care of one's person and equipment.*

3   Plugs and Wobblers                                                 18
    *World-wide plug and wobbler types and their manufacturers
    and originators. How they are made and the adjustments to
    keep them fishing correctly. The various techniques that can be
    used to ensure they are fished in accordance with their design.*

4   Homemade Spinners                                                  32
    *How to make and fish your own spinners, with advice on repairs
    and improvements to commercial lures.*

5   Commercial Spinners                                                39
    *Details of international lures, their manufacturers, how they are
    made, species of fish and the types of water for which they can
    be used.*

6   More Spinners                                                      49
    *More international manufacturers and their products, types of
    lures and fishing advice.*

7   Light Spinners and Fly Spinners                                    59
    *Amateur and commercial designs, how to make and fish them.
    How they can be used both on light spinning or fly-fishing
    equipment.*

8   Fly-fishing Tackle                                                 68
    *Fly rods and lines with the other items which make for a well-
    equipped fly-fisher. Some advice on reading the water and
    conditions.*

  9   Fly Lure Tying Techniques                                          72
         *Materials and tools needed. Tying instructions for hacklewings,*
         *hairwings, leadheads, tubes, deerhair heads and tandem hook*
         *mounts.*

 10   Fly Lures                                                          78
         *Materials, patterns, plastic waggle tails, fishing and tying*
         *techniques.*

 11   More Fly Lures                                                     91
         *International patterns and, where known, their originators.*
         *Tying techniques, types of water and fishing advice.*

 12   Leadheads, Poppers and Others                                     104
         *Floating lures, fast sinking lure patterns including many specials.*
         *Fishing and tying tips for all types.*

# List of Plates

1   Rapala: Countdown; Sliver-Jointed; Jointed
2   Rapala: Floating; Rattl'n Rap; Fat Rap; Shad Rap
3   Big 'S' Plugs, assorted sizes
4   Plugs: Tomic Plugs; Canadian Wigglers
5   Home-made Spoons and Spinners with fly tails
6   Bar-Spinners with home-made tails
7   Minnows: Lane minnows and Dexter minnows
8   Landa Lures: Lukki, Herri and Pikko
9   Mepps: Aglia, Mini Saumon; Gold TW; Silver TW
10  Delta: Assorted Flasha Spoons
11  Spoons: Dexter Wedge, Ogwen, Menal, Long Spoon, Conway Spoon,
    Mepps Syclops, Ragot's Yann Spoon
12  Plastic Tail Fly Lures: Black Lure, Yellow Cree Lure, Tadpole, Yellow
    Wiggler, Damsel Wiggler, Orange Lure, Green Badger Lure, White
    Wiggler, Bloodworm

# Acknowledgements

My book would have been extremely difficult to complete without the help of a number of people. My thanks and appreciation go to the following and their companies for information given, with my special thanks to those who sent photographs or samples of their products to provide some of the illustrations. Alan Bramley, Partridge of Redditch Ltd; Jean Luc Faure, Mepps S.A., Contes, France; Vince Lister, Berkshire; H.D. Marshman, H. Turrall & Co Ltd, Devon; Tony Perrin, Landa Sport, Lancashire; Herbert Guillios, Ragot S.A., Loudeac, France; Peter Williams, Carmarthen, Wales; Donald Glass, Fife, Scotland; Kay Potter, Bruce & Walker Ltd, Cambridgeshire; R.I. Brightwell, Abu Garcia (UK) Ltd; Pertti Rautio, Rapala Oy, Vaaksy, Finland; A.A. Baxter, Farlow's London; James L. Hardy, House of Hardy, Alnwick; John Bailey, Dan Bailey's Fly Shop, Montana, USA; John Lane, G.M. Lane & Co, Limerick, Ireland; S. Morris, Morris Nicholson Cartwright Ltd, Altrincham; John L. Tomsett, Shakespeare Company (UK) Ltd; Alan Hildebrandt, John J. Hildebrandt Corporation, Indiana, USA; Arnold Lindquist, Lindquist Bros. Bait Co Ltd, Ontario, Canada; Nigel E.N. Neville-Jones, Lures Direct, Dorset; Tom Moss, Tomic, Vancouver Island, British Columbia, Canada; A.G. Westmoreland, Dexter Products Company, Llanfairfechan, Wales; Henry McConnell, Delta Tackle, Plymouth; O. Thomas and J. Mitchell, Normark Sport Ltd, Newton Abbot, Devon.

My special thanks to my old friends Gordon Bellman, for the superb work producing all but two of the illustrations and Dave Clark, Chris Martindale, Trevor Sobey and Michael Shephard for their help testing my prototypes over the years. Finally my thanks to Sue Coley for sorting out much of my manuscript in her usual skilful way.

*S.M. Veale*
*1992*

# Introduction

This selection of international spinning and fly lures is intended as a guide for the sport angler wishing to go freshwater fishing anywhere throughout the world with rod and line.

Freshwater lures comprise many types and their construction can be of any material, ranging from the all-metal spinners or wooden wobbling types right across the artificial lure spectrum to the fly lures which are made of fur and feather.

Most of the lures given can be used, and in many instances are used very successfully, in waters many thousands of miles from where they first saw the light of day.

Many of the lures are from well-known international manufacturers from both the European and North American continents. For most of the professional products, I have given brief details of their manufacturers and of their various lures, including methods of construction, materials and techniques used in their production, and, where known, details of their originators.

I have not forgotten the do-it-yourself enthusiasts who like to make their own tackle and perhaps who design their own artificial spinners and lures for fresh-water fishing. For the do-it-yourself fishermen and others who wish to broaden their horizons, I have compiled a comprehensive selection of easy-to-make lures, mounts or spinners — many of my own design. Full instructions are given on how to make them, including fly-dressing techniques and the materials required; and finally fishing methods for these lures and the species of fish for which they were designed.

My own fly lure and spinning lure patterns are the result of years of experimentation in design and practical use in fishing trips by myself and friends.

The lures have only really been comprehensively tested on the various trout species and salmon, with the occasional pike or perch fishing trip, although on game fishing trips I have taken the odd dace or grayling with them.

I am sure such a comprehensive choice of professional and amateur lures will present some difficulty to the beginner in deciding which type to use and where. To help the novice to make the correct selection and to assist their presentation of their choice to the fish, I have given details on the most suitable water and weather conditions for the various lure types, together with detailed fishing advice and many of the techniques which may prove successful.

Fishing tips, fly-tying and construction tips for artificial baits are given through-out this book and I hope these will encourage more fishermen to widen their outlook on the sport, particularly those fishermen at each end of the spectrum who have adopted fixed positions: the purist fly-fisher and the die-hard bait-fisher — natural or live-bait.

Good luck and good fishing.

*S. Michael Veale*
*1992*

# 1

# Spinners and Hooks

It is said that the early lures were made and used by the natives of the North American continent. These primitive lures apparently consisted of fur and feather with bone hooks. The method of fishing them was either jigging in ice holes, fishing from canoes or from the shore.

I don't know when the first metal and wooden spinning lures were used. There is a delightful little story of a miller sitting by the water eating his food when he accidently dropped his spoon into the water. As he watched the spoon fluttering to the bottom a fish darted forward and struck it. The date when this happened and the individual concerned is rather hazy. No doubt the miller or somebody at that time realised the significance of this event, assuming this account of the story is accurate.

At the start of the nineteenth century, anglers used live or dead baits of small fish which were mounted on spinning mounts. These natural baits were fished in a variety of methods: trolling or trailing behind a moving boat or punt; casting out on rod and line and stripping the line back to fish the lure; casting the bait and retrieving using the sink and draw technique; jigging the lure from boat or bank.

There is not a great deal of difference between the bait-spinning mounts of today and the mounts of yesteryear, except perhaps the number of hooks and their quality.

The earliest recorded reference I have seen concerning the artificial spinner was by Delabera P. Blaine, in his book *An Encyclopedia of Rural Sports*, dated 1840. This spinner was called 'Devil Bait' and was constructed from an unknown flexible material which had the advantage of allowing it to be adjusted for fast or slow rotation speeds, which compared favourably with the bait-spinning mounts. Its size and shape was the same as the natural minnow with plenty of gold and silver tinsel to give it a fish-like glitter. It had a multi-hook mount in the same way as the bait-spinning mount and was fished apparently in the same way.

I think it will be safe to assume this spinner was first devised in the early part of the nineteenth century. By all accounts it was popular and quite successful, hence its name 'Devil Bait'. There is no doubt this lure was one of the forerunners of the artificial spinner.

One of the early manufacturers of quality spinning baits in the nineteenth century was Hardy Bros of Alnwick. At the turn of the century they were producing a range of quality spinning lures which were unique: the list consists of such famous lures as the Halcyon Spinner, Pioneer Devons, the Pennell Minnow, Hardy's Transparent Amber Devons, Hardy's Quill Minnow, the Silk Phantom, Soleskin Phantom, Rubber Phantom, Hardy's 'Horn' Phantoms, Excelsior Spinner, and various spoons. It is a pity that some of these spinners are no longer available. I remember over thirty-five years ago being given two Hardy's Transparent Amber Devons size two (5 cm) by an old fisherman. These spinners proved quite deadly for sea trout in clear water, they would come from across the river to hit them. As with all spinners over a period of time, wear and tear and losses took their toll; I never did find any suitable replacements.

The spinners available today can be classified in the following groups: Bar-Spinners, Devon Minnows, Spoons, Wobblers, Plugs, Quill Minnows, Fly-Spinners, and Wooden Spoons.

### Bar-Spinners

The bar-spinner is made up of a stainless steel shaft of wire which at one end is twisted into a loop in which is placed the treble hook; then the body weight is slid down the wire shaft followed by a coloured bead. Next is the clevis which is first hooked into the spinning blade and then slid down the wire shaft, followed by another bead. The wire is now twisted to form the eye to which the fishing line is tied. The bead acts rather like a bearing for the spinning motion of the blade. It is not necessary for the treble hook to be secured directly on the spinner shaft, as a split ring can be used to join the treble hook to the bottom loop of the spinner. The split ring makes it possible for quick changes of hooks and fly patterns dressed on trebles. Any manufacturer's spinner, after having the original hook damaged, can be changed to this method: cut off the original damaged hook, and add a split ring and replacement treble. When buying bar-spinners or any spinner always check the hooks, as unfortunately not all manufacturers pay enough attention in this department.

### Devon Minnows

Devons are available in the following types:
Classic Devons: lightweight or heavyweight.
Spratts Devon: lightweight or heavyweight.
Wooden Devons: standard.
Metal Devons: heavyweight or standard.
Sprey Devons: normal or heavyweight.
Plastic Devons: various.
Devon Minnows are normally made in only three different materials. For the amateur tackle-maker the wooden Devon can be produced quite easily by being turned out on a lathe or carved by hand. The hook trace for the minnow is passed through the centre of the body shell to enable the complete spinner to be tied to the fishing line. This trace consists of Alasticum wire which is passed through the treble hook eye and twisted to form the wire shaft, then a plastic bead or tulip is slid down to the hook. The other end of the wire is passed through a good quality swivel and secured, thus completing the Devon spinning mount.

For the enthusiast, Devon minnow shells in various materials can be acquired unpainted which will allow for painting any special designs. It is possible for the wooden Devon maker to fit fins in a manner which produces slower rotation speeds. It will be necessary to experiment with the different positions of the fins to achieve the rotation speed desired. To make a heavyweight wooden Devon add a copper tube throughout its length, and try to balance your Devons so that they swim in the horizontal plane – not tail down.

## Spoons

The spoon-spinner for the amateur tackle maker is probably one of the most simple to make. The tools needed are a pair of metal snips, file, hammer, small drill and a vice. From a block of wood carve a mould using a tablespoon as a model to acquire the correct shape; this can be varied according to the designer's specifications.

Cut the spoon shape required from a sheet of copper, place in the mould and hammer to shape. Not only does the hammering give the spoon its shape, it also gives it an uneven finish which means the light is reflected from it at many angles and adds to its attraction. Next drill a hole each end of the spoon, add a split ring with a treble hook at one end and a split ring with a swivel attached on the other; now it is ready for a swim. Tackle-making, as in fly-tying, is very satisfying when fish are taken on lures which you have made yourself. Later in the book I will be dealing with the various commercial spoons so I will leave the descriptions of the various types till then.

## Wobblers

Wobblers are designed to swim on the horizontal plane with a fish-imitating action. Their construction can be of wood, plastic or metal. There are quite a number of commercially-made models which I will be dealing with later.

For the amateur tackle-maker the construction of your own wobblers can be quite a challenge. They can be carved out of pieces of wood and dressed on plastic tubes with foam rubber using fly-tying techniques. With some of the designs, particularly those on tubes, it will be necessary to place some weight on the lower side of the tube to ensure that it swims correctly, i.e. the right way up. (Later I will give full details how to apply the tying methods.) The most difficult aspect of producing your own wobblers is making them swim correctly and I have no short cuts. You will have to make the lure and test it in the water tank and adjust it until you are completely happy with its swimming pattern.

## Plugs

Plugs can be divided into four modes, deep-diving plugs, floating plugs, shallow-diving plugs, surface-popping and sinking plugs. Plugs for floating and surface fishing are made of wood or plastic with the natural buoyancy these materials give. Floating plugs are designed for shallow-diving and just under the surface fishing; most poppers are designed to be fished slowly along the surface and retrieved back to the angler in small jerks, 'popping' them so as to cause a disturbance on the water's surface. They are useful for fishing under bankside vegetation. Sinking plugs are for deep water where weight is needed to present the plug to the fish, down at the correct fishing depth. Deep-diving plugs, whether floating or sinking, can be recognised by their long wide metal or plastic lip which will drive them quickly under the water when the retrieve is started.

When buying commercially-produced plugs do give them a good check; while there are many good designs available, there are designs being offered which do not really come up to the standard required. Points to look for in a quality plug are: vane and eye ring in line; treble hooks heavy enough to deal with the species of fish the plug is designed to take. Check the anchor points for the hook hangers, tail and belly; if they are held in by screws make sure they are tight and not likely to pull out.

Plug design for the amateur tackle-maker probably gives him the widest scope of all the wooden lures, and he can let his fancy run free. To make a plug, first select a piece of fine grain wood or part of an old broom handle about three inches long (8 cm). Drill a hole in the centre of the wood throughout its length. Then drill two short holes in what is going to be the plug's belly. To carry out this operation you will need to hold the wood firmly in a vice. When drilling the wood length-wise, it may be better to drill from both ends and try to make the holes meet in the middle. The two belly holes will need to meet up with the lengthwise centre hole. The inside of these holes should be waterproofed with a sealing agent. Fashion the plug to your specifications using a coarse rasp and finishing off with sandpaper. Cut the sloping forehead and slot for the vane. Now fit the main wire with the belly hook holders. These holders consist of two swivels which are pushed into the belly, carefully lining the eyes so that the wire can be pushed through the middle of the plug, and secured in place. This operation can be a little tricky and needs patience. Form the loop eyes in the main wire fore and aft and seal the hook holders and loop eye with plastic wood. Fix the vane and use split rings for hanging the trebles. Now, the moment of truth: test the plug in the water tank before painting. This will give the swimming pattern and allow any adjustments or corrections to the design to be made, either to the body or the vane. First paint with primer, then follow it with the final coat. To achieve a fish scale effect, spray through a relatively fine gauze screen. The whole lot can be completed with a coat of polyurethane to give the final finish to the lure.

**Quill Minnows**
A simple but very effective design, particularly for sea trout fishing. To construct your quill minnow take a quill from a goose or turkey wing, selecting it carefully for shape, and cut to the size required. Cut the narrow tip where the treble hook will be and ensure that the inside of the quill is clear. At the end of the quill, which is going to be the head, cut a slot for about a quarter of the quill's length. Make a wire mount similar to the type made for the Devon minnow. Slide this mount through the centre of the quill with the end of the swivel poking just clear of the quill. The spinning fins should be of plastic or metal and in one piece, cut to a butterfly nut shape with each end of the wing bent or moulded to form the fins. The fins are fashioned in opposite directions; for fast or slow spin the designer will have to experiment. Push the fins into the slot already cut into the quill and whip with silk and varnish. Minnows can be painted any colours.

Later I will be giving full details of fishing the quill minnow in small and rough streams.

**Fly-Spinners**
A fly-spinner in my view is the most effective clear water spinner available, particularly in low water during the summer. Later in the book I will be giving fly-spinner patterns and fly wobblers. Basic construction of the fly-spinner can take many forms; I prefer a bar-spinner or spoon with a fly-tail.

## Wooden Spoons

Carving of wooden spoons is for the enthusiast and skilled wood carver. With care and skill, fine wooden spoons can be produced in all shapes and sizes. Close grained woods are the most suitable to work with for the amateur wood carver. The finished spoon should be given several coats of paint; most fluorescent colours will give the spoon a good finish.

When fishing the wooden spoon in some conditions it will be necessary to add weight to the fishing line to give it some depth. The weight should be a metre (3 ft) away from the spoon on a breakaway point. This will give the spoon freedom of movement and allow it to twist and tumble in the current.

The lively movement of the wooden spoon in swift flowing water makes it an extremely good fish catcher, particularly if you replace the treble hook with a treble hook fly pattern. This will certainly impart additional life to the spoon.

## Hooks

It was in the early part of the nineteenth century that Redditch started to develop into a major centre for producing fishing tackle in the United Kingdom. One of the early hook-makers was Polycarp Allcock, the father of Samuel Allcock who founded the famous company of S. Allcock Ltd. Another early hook-maker in Redditch was Edwin Partridge, whose grandson Albert Partridge, became well known whilst running the business from 1910 until the 1940s. Early in 1923 Albert Partridge moved the business into its present premises and in 1933, A.E. Partridge and Sons became a limited company. During 1970 Alan Bramley joined the company and in 1982 he became a major shareholder and changed the company name to Partridge of Redditch Ltd.

Of all the old hook-makers, Partridges are the only company to have survived the commercial trials and pressures of the last thirty years. Famous UK companies such as Edgar Sealey, Allcocks, Bernard Sealey and Millwards have all gone out of hand hook-making or have disappeared altogether. Partridges, as well as many other hook-makers, produced their hook points using the traditional Redditch method of grinding round points on hooks rather than cutting them. Although the round points on hooks produced using this method have been sharp and generally did not turn over, Alan Bramley felt they could be improved on in most of the range of hooks produced, simply by redesigning the geometry of the points.

In 1980 Partridge started to shorten the points on many of their hooks. The big advantage of this innovation is that it allows the angler to set the hook beyond the bard much more quickly and with less effort, hopefully cutting some fish losses. The process of forming the hook points now took longer with three or more passes over the grinding stone. This ensured the new design had points of the new geometry with the very sharp tips and adequate thickness behind them to support the finest of points and give them strength. The taper in the point changed several times before it levelled into the main diameter of the wire at the point where the barb is cut.

Partridges use a high carbon steel wire for the bulk of their hook production. This wire is harder than most, thereby allowing a really sharp point to be formed which initially remains largely unaffected by the subsequent stages. One advantage with hard carbon steel wire is that should the hook point be damaged in any way, the point can easily be sharpened back to a needle-sharp tip.

Because of the special qualities of high carbon Sheffield steel wire, hooks made with it have extremely sharp points and maintain their sharpness even after plenty of use. However, Alan Bramley in his quest for perfection at a reasonable price started looking at technology in other areas. As a 'wet' shaver he was impressed by the improvements made by razor blade manufacturers in prolonging the life of the cutting edge of their products. On investigation he found the secret lay in a PTFE (polytetrafluoroethylene) coating, which gave an even but low friction covering to the blade. Unfortunately there were two big disadvantages to PTFE on its own for fishing hook protection. Firstly it had to be applied at temperatures which could effect the temper of the hook. Secondly it was not in itself a protection against rust (rusty hooks have always been a problem), and the point was put to Alan Bramley that perhaps stainless steel wire would be the answer.

Alan's reply was: 'For cost reasons, many of the very special stainless and alloy steels would not be suitable for fish hooks. Many of these steels are twenty times more expensive than carbon steels. Equally these special steels would not be available in the relatively small quantities which we would need. The stainless steel wire that is therefore economically available for fish hook production will not heat treat to give the same strength that we can achieve with high carbon steel wire. Furthermore stainless steel hooks do not hold their points for anything like as long as high carbon steel.'

With his team, Alan Bramley continued his quest for a method of applying PTFE to carbon steel fish hooks and at the same time looking for a good rust resistant material, which could be combined with PTFE to provide good rust protection to carbon steel hooks and give a surface covering with the benefit of low friction which would prolong the life of the hook in any situation.

Later Alan's quest was successful and he reports: 'It was some time afterwards that my search led me to the British invention of Niflor. This is a surface coating which can be readily applied to carbon steel and combines the corrosion resistance of nickel/phosphorous with the special qualities of PTFE.'

Alan continues: 'The only problem which the coating appeared to present was the dull grey colour. I could not conceive that the "traditional" angler would accept a grey hook, but I have been surprised. Anglers who have seen the grey hooks find that they are less obtrusive and for the fly dresser, the neutral grey enhances rather than clashes with the colours of the fly.'

Niflor coating is used for the treatment of metals in all sorts of industrial situations, giving long life protection particularly in harsh and saltwater environments. The PTFE particles are evenly distributed in the nickel/phosphorous thus resulting in an even, dry-lubricated, low friction slippery surface which is extremely hard and resistant to wear. Fishing hooks which have been treated with Niflor have a hard corrosion-resistant finish all over the hook, which defeats the rust – particularly behind the barb, always the weak spot on any hook.

Making a fish hook by hand involves several stages. First, a piece of high carbon Sheffield steel wire is straightened and cut to length. For all double hooks and most single hooks, points are formed at each end of the wire on the grindstone. Double hooks, these have the advantage of being formed from the single length of wire. For single hooks it is cut in half – thus making two hooks. Treble hooks are formed by brazing a double and single together.

After the point is formed the barb is now cut in at the back of the point. The next step is to place the wire in the bending former and shape the wire to the hook size. Hook eyes are formed by bowing the tail of the shank (in the case of the single hook) around a small stud on a hand press and set up or down. Many ranges of hooks are cold forged in the heel of the bend for extra strength. The hooks are heat-treated in a controlled atmosphere and tempered. Some ranges of hooks go through a process which chemically sharpens the tip of the point. After chemical cleaning the hooks can be bronzed or blacked by hand or plated with special finishes such as Niflor, gold, nickel, or bright tin.

All Partridge hooks are inspected before being dispatched. Treble hooks, normally in black finish, can be made available in all other finishes if required.

**Partridge X1 Outpoint Treble** General purpose treble hook with outward turned short points, small barbs and strong forged bends. Superb hook for all situations from replacement hook on spinners to making prawn and shrimp mounts. Use with Waddington shanks and tube flies.

**Rob Wilson CS9 Outpoint Treble** Similar to Code X1 but made in 2X stronger wire. Rob Wilson of Brora in Scotland identified the need for heavy hooks for big fish and high water conditions. Same general use as the Code X1, useful for big pike rigs.

**Partridge X3 Needleeye Treble** Designed for tube flies, useful for second hook on tandem mount. Outpoint with small barbs.

**Partridge X2B Longshank Salmon Treble** Suitable fly patterns can be dressed directly on it. On the smaller sizes, sea trout and trout flies can be dressed. Useful for second hook on tandem mounts.

*Partridge Treble Hooks*

# 2

# Fishing the Spinning Lure

Tremendous progress in the development of equipment and improvement of techniques have been made since spinning was first practised in the last century. Early spinning tackle consisted of long heavy rods and centre pin reels. The spinning line was usually a dressed silk line. Undressed plaited silk lines of 18 to 30 lb (8·17–13·62 kg) were also available which could be used according to the reel and circumstances. It was necessary to coat the undressed line with one of the line dopes; failure to do so would result in the line sticking to the adjacent coils when being cast and causing all sorts of problems. Before the fishing reel was invented, the dressed spinning line was cast from the coils held in the hand, or from coils laid out on a line tray strapped to the waist. If the angler was boat fishing, the fishing line would be coiled in the boat.

I remember many years ago, as a lad, I watched an old fisherman spinning using a centre pin reel with a long rod and a massive brass Devon minnow. What he did was to strip the line off the reel and coil it in his hand; when ready he cast it out, with the brass Devon hitting the water with a loud thump. He then spun the minnow back by stripping the line back slowly, forming the coils in his hand ready for the next cast. He then repeated the process, fishing the spinner slow and deep, which is very important in high cold river conditions.

The next important step in reel design was the free running wooden Nottingham reel, followed by reels such as the Hardy Bros Silex reel, where the spinner could be cast straight off the reel and spun in by winding the reel. It was claimed at that time if the sportsman followed the instruction for the Silex correctly it was possible to master the casting technique within a half-hour of practice. The cast is made underhand; it must be smooth and even as jerky movements or keeping the finger too long on lever will cause tangles and overruns. When winding ensure there is no kinking or twisting of line and its action is pleasant and smooth. To enjoy good casting the spinning line may be of any make, but must be smooth and pliant. The most important point is that the coils must not stick together. If the line is right it will fall off the reel as it unwinds.

An interesting item I noticed in Hardy Brothers catalogue of 1902 was: 'On Saturday October 8th 1898 at the Gresham Angling Society's tournament, J.T. Emery using a 2½ oz [70 g] bait, a "Hardy" Murdoch steel-centre built cane rod and a "Hardy" patent "Silex" winch succeeded in reaching the enormous distance of 87 yards 2 feet [81 metres]. This is the world's greatest record for casting direct from the reel reported.'

In 1897 an American watchmaker Henry Shakespeare, the founder of the Shakespeare Corporation invented and patented the first level-wind mechanism for multipliers. American multipliers, though they cast well and were free running, needed to have the line guided manually to ensure a level spread on the reel drum.

The next spinning reels which came on the scene were of the fixed spool design. The Illingworth and Hardy's Altex come to mind. It was the fixed-spool reel which, because it did not take long to learn to cast long distances and its indiscriminate use by a small minority, caused some bad feeling. Spinning in all its modes is a very skilful form of angling – it is not the case of throwing the spinner out and raking it back. Admittedly it is a lot easier learning to handle a rod and fixed-spool reel than it is a fly rod and reel. However once the mechanical application of being able to handle the equipment has been mastered, the real learning process now begins: to achieve the ability to apply the mechanical skills of handling the spinner or fly on the end of the line skilfully in all types of water.

Spinning in rivers should only be practised when the time of year and water conditions dictate. The only exception to this is the type of water where fly-fishing is impossible or very difficult, then of course it is up to the angler to use whatever method that is suitable. If for example you fish rivers that are very heavily wooded or have steep cliff faces forming the banks, spinning or bait fishing are probably the only way to fish them. This is the type of rivers that I fish, although there are the odd pools where it is possible to fly-fish, very useful for night fishing when the sea trout are running.

When spinning in high water conditions in a medium-sized river, it is not simply a case of having the ability to drop a spinner between overhanging branches a few inches from the opposite bank. The first thing for the angler to decide is which spinner is most suitable. If the flow of water is very strong the weight of the spinner needs to be adequate, making it possible for the lure to swim at the right depth and speed and on a horizontal plane. Any spinner swimming incorrectly – or four times too fast – will not as a rule take fish. This is where the throw-and-chance-it brigade fall down (apart from the occasional accident when they hook the odd suicidal fish). Unfortunately this is one of the areas of spinning where they give the responsible conservation-minded fishermen who spin a poor press. It is highly irresponsible to continue spinning for game fish when you are catching nothing except small trout and parr; even if they are returned the damage has been done, particularly when the smolts are making their trip to the sea in May. Spinning must only be practised in game-fishing rivers when water conditions are right, or there is plenty of game fish in the pools.

Most experienced anglers even on strange waters can spot some of the salmon lies by studying the water. However, knowledge of the water to be fished gives an advantage to the angler who knows the lies and taking places. If fishing on strange water the best way to fish the pools is to start spinning in the neck of the pool. The spinner is cast across to the slack water on the far side. A few turns of the reel will bring the spinner into the faster flow; let the rough water take the spinning lure and fish it around while you keep a taut line with the odd turn of the reel handle, thus making the current work the lure. As the direction of the line indicates that the spinner is entering the quiet water near the bank, increase your reeling to keep the bait fishing and do not allow it to go to the bottom. Very often as the spinner comes around in a curve the take will come; raise your rod and the fish should be on. After each cast, take two or three paces downstream ready for the next cast. By working down the pool systematically all the salmon lies are covered. Very often, by fishing back up to the pool again, a couple of paces at a time casting as you go, a fish, which perhaps unknown to you, had moved too but not taken spinner the first time, now takes it firmly. This ploy is always worth trying. Too many times have I seen another rod follow down a pool a few minutes after the first, and have a fish catch hold. Sometimes I have been the victim, other times I have been the one with the 'smile'.

Passing on now to a typical day's salmon fishing in the autumn, at the end of the season. The leaves have changed colour and are falling off the trees. It has been raining for several days, the river is running high and slightly coloured, bringing down all the debris which has accumulated during the long dry summer months. The autumn gales blowing the leaves off the trees and the rain washing them into the river, makes spinning very difficult. It is very frustrating to catch leaves on your triangles every other cast.

Move on to the bank and carefully study the water, trying to decide how best to tackle the conditions for these late running salmon. Firstly the rod must be suitable for salmon and not less than nine foot (2·74 metres). As the river we are fishing is small and rocky, the fixed-spool reel will be ideal. The river is quite high and the flowing strongly; if you are to avoid the line kinking (because at times the lure will be spinning very fast) it is important to have a good quality swivel joining the trace to the fishing line and if necessary an anti-kink vane on the line.

Considering the height, speed and colour of the water in front of you, it is best if you start with a slow spin heavy yellow belly Devon minnow. It is important to fish deep. The slow spin of the brown and yellow Devon as it is fished across the river will give an intermittent yellow flash. A faster action spinner in this fast current would not give a distinct flash and therefore would not be as effective. Fishing every likely lie, slowly continue up the river. Because the water is slightly coloured it is not possible to see all the rocks and boulders on the river bed. In high water the only indication of an obstruction under the surface is the disturbance to the surface of the water. With experience you will soon recognise this flow pattern. Cast your spinner first on the lower side and fish the water and then with care do the same on the higher side of this underwater rock. When the salmon are running, rocks of this type make temporary resting places and you may be lucky to find a fish in residence who will oblige and catch hold. Leaving the fast deep run behind, you are now on the wider part of the river; it is shallower here, the flow faster and the water clearer. Because of the changed water conditions it pays now to change spinners. As you can see the river bed and the rocks, this makes spoon fishing practical. Change the Devon minnow for a black and gold spoon. Cast the spoon straight across but slightly upstream, dropping it neatly near the opposite bank. Allow the current to take the spoon tumbling with it, but keeping it on a tight line. Start the retrieve, hugging the spoon close to the river bed; any undulations of the river bed will not interfere with the spoon. The current and the tight line should cause the spoon to ride over them like a well sprung car. With weed beds and rocks it will be necessary to raise your rod and take the spoon off the bottom to avoid snagging. After fishing this wide fast rocky part of the river you come to a narrow neck which, because of the height of water, is unfishable. Now move on to the first main pool where the water flow is considerably slower but quite murky. The best tactic now is to change the spoon for a wobbler. A fluorescent orange and yellow articulated wobbler would probably give the best chance of being seen in these conditions. (How to fish wobblers and plugs is described in detail later.)

I expect you are wondering why I have not made mention of the bar-spinner during our autumn day's fishing. The reason for this is quite simple, the river was too high for effective bar-spinner fishing. To cast the bar-spinner into high or very fast water means that when trying to retrieve, it comes to the surface or fishes very high in the water. When retrieving it against the force of the water it is rather like playing a small fish; the rod is bent over and recovering the line makes the winch work hard; the clutch sometimes slips. I have seen anglers fishing bar-spinners in unsuitable conditions with large weights on their line and heavy, stiff rods able to drag this lot back against the current in an attempt to fish deep. In my opinion this is not how spinning should be practised, and the exponents of this method are missing a great deal. It must be very difficult for them to make their lures fish properly. Spinning is a highly skilled branch of angling and experienced anglers will always adjust their methods to prevailing conditions. As I have demonstrated, conditions over a short stretch of river in flood will differ quite considerably. This is also true for non flood conditions, however perhaps not quite so dramatically; the deep pools and glides and shallow runs are still there, only the flow of water is less.

Let us now move on to the following year. The time is mid-July, fortunately there has been some rain and the river is running at a good level – deep and green. The sea trout are running and water conditions are good for spinning. The rod must be at least nine feet (2·74 metres), rather more sensitive than the rod used for the autumn salmon, but powerful enough to deal with summer salmon.

Starting at the same place as you did last October, stand a while and study the water. The scene is vastly different, a warm overcast day; the river is a reasonable height showing the greenish colour which is ideal for spinning. The bankside vegetation is bright green and in full flower; the trees, heavily leaved, sway gently in the breeze; the birds add their harmonic notes to the music of running water tinkling over the stones; the buzzard hawks circle overhead, their shrill cries hanging on the air, a beautiful day – certainly different from last October.

Select a medium-sized copper bar-spinner and fish the first long deep glide, carefully making every possible use of the bankside vegetation to give cover from the fish. Sea trout are very shy – if they see you first you don't see them.

The first stretch completed, with nothing doing, you now come to where the river widens, the water is shallow and the current runs fast. There are some very good lies for sea trout among the rocks. Change the bar-spinner now for a small copper spoon where the treble is dressed with a cock hackle dyed hot orange. This is deadly for taking sea trout out of relatively fast water in these rocky lies; fish the spoon as described previously. Moving on, you now come to the narrow neck where the water rushes through. No need to hide from the fish here, the natural disturbance and turbulence of the water will conceal you. After changing the fly-spoon for a heavy gold bar-spinner, carefully prepare to tackle the difficult fast water. Fishing this type of water is an area where tackle losses can be expected; sometimes a little luck is needed to avoid the rocks in this fast water – rocks you cannot see clearly, but provide cover for the fish lying behind them in hollows sheltered from the fast water. It is very difficult to present the lure correctly. There is always a chance of a salmon in this type of water and the tactic here is to cast the spinner upstream to one side of the large rocks. It must be thrown far enough upstream to enable the lure to sink deep enough to be fished back beside the rock and then curled in behind it. Because of the flow of the water the spinner is travelling fast and you will have to wind vigorously to keep in touch and not allow the lure to bury itself in the bottom. Difficult spinning – but very exciting – especially when you see a fish chasing your spinner downwards at speed and take it as it curls back to you at the end of the retrieve.

After fishing the narrow exit from the big pool now move up on to the pool. To fish this pool it is best to start at the top and fish down using the tactics as described previously. The choice of spinners is rather more difficult; all the spinners will work well in the moderate flow and there is plenty of depth. Colour is the most important consideration. I would try a blue/silver or green/gold wobbler or spoon. After you have fished down the pool with one type and colour lure, it is worth fishing down again trying a different lure and colour. Remember, do not fish too fast and get that lure deep. In rivers game fish lie in recognised lies except when they are active; then they could be anywhere.

Trolling is a useful method of taking fish in the big freshwater lakes of Scotland, Ireland and elsewhere in the world where these waters exist. My experience of trolling is rather limited although I have considerable freshwater boat fishing experience.

The equipment for trolling wobblers or spinning lures is basically the same as river fishing; the rods can be a little shorter and stiffer depending on the species being fished. The multiplier reel is probably best for most situations, particularly for long lines where good control is required.

Depth control of the trolling lure is vital. This can be achieved by trolling various lengths of line; the longer the line the deeper the lure will swim. It may require some experimenting to determine the correct line length for the depth required. With buoyant lures, weights on the line will be necessary to achieve the fishing depth. The weight should be a metre (3 ft) in front of the lure; again it will be necessary to adjust weights to find the correct amount to enable the lure to be fished at the depth where the fish are suspected to be. When trolling pay particular attention to the headlands and underwater reefs; if you have a boatman with you who knows the water your problems are over, he will place you in the most productive areas and probably tell you what lure to use. However if you are on your own it will be necessary to study the water and tactics.

It is best to start trolling in the shallow waters close to the shore, paying particular attention to any headland before swinging into the bays. Start at a slow speed – have about 15 metres (16 yd) of line out. This should give the lure depth of two to four metres (6½–13 ft) depending a little on the trolling speed. When trolling the shallows the longer the trolling line the better to avoid putting down the fish in clear water. During cold water periods the very slow speed will be most effective. By varying the speed you will soon discover the most productive one.

Considerable success can be had trolling large fly lures. The equipment needed is a powerful fly rod, strong enough to withstand the drag of the trolling line and deep fishing the lead line or super fast sinking fly-line. If the boat fly-fisherman wishes to mix his day's traditional fishing methods with some gentle rowing while trolling with the same equipment, all that he needs to do is to add weight to his leader and, instead of casting his lure, pay it out while rowing until he has achieved the length required. Some of the fly lures for this type of fishing are very large and later in the book I will give many dressings suitable for this mode.

Knowing the depth of the water is one of the most important requirements for the trolling enthusiast, not just the water he is covering at that time, but over as much of the water as possible – so that he knows the underwater contours where the ledges, ridges and deeps are. If you have not got a boatman with indispensable local knowledge, the next best thing is an echo sounder. If used as the manufacturer's instructions it will give you the full contours of the bed of the lake you happen to be sitting over. This will make sure you are only fishing productive water; also shoals of fish will show on the sounder which will give you a knowledge of the favoured parts of the water for the various species. Another aid for the angler in lieu of a boatman is the outboard or electric motor. The outboard motor is more useful for the big water where its noise perhaps is not too much of a nuisance. On smaller waters or where the peace and quiet of the surroundings are appreciated, then the electric motor is preferable, unless you are fond of rowing – I must admit I don't mind watching my boat partner doing the rowing.

The echo sounder would also be an asset when spinning from the boat. The best tactic is to hug the shoreline of the lake, fishing towards the shore. Drop the spinner a few metres from the shore line, fish it back, at the same time allowing the spinner to follow the contour of the shelving bottom, going deeper until the cast is fished out. For working a gravel slope, anchor your boat in the shallow water, cast the spinner as far as necessary and then work it back from the deep water to the shallows. To fish a rocky reef or gravel bar, approach it from the upwind side and anchor the boat a long cast off. Casting as far as possible so that the spinning lure lands just beyond the ridge, fish it back in the shallows at the crown of the ridge. This can at times be very productive. Another very productive area is where feeder streams run into a lake. Special attention needs to be given here, particularly at the back end of the season. Big brown trout which have been hiding in the depths all year, will gather at these inlets prior to their spawning runs, feeding on the fry. This is probably the only time you may get on terms with them. Good runs of salmon and sea trout pass through lakes which are part of a waterway where the lake drains via the river to the sea. The inlets and outlets are good fishing areas when the fish are entering or leaving the lake on their journey to the spawning beds.

Remember when boat fishing, safety is the number one priority. Make sure your boat is properly equipped with lifebelts and an anchor and that the oars can be locked in the rowlocks and cannot fall into the water if you let them go. On big waters be doubly careful; if you have a boatman there will be no problem but if you are fishing without local knowledge at hand, check the weather before going out. Conditions on large freshwater lakes can change in minutes from a quiet gentle ripple to metre-high waves or more. If you think I am over dramatizing I will give you an account of an incident which happened nearly twenty years ago. A friend and I decided to fish a local lake one Saturday. The shape of this lake was rather like a frying pan except the handle was twice as thick. The best area for fish was the shallow area right across the top third of the pan. We were fishing in this area when the wind very quickly became stronger, blowing from the top of the pan straight down the handle, pushing up a very heavy chop on the water. We decided it would be a good idea to make for the nearest bank and land. This was a mistake. As the boat was turned broadside onto the wind we quickly started shipping water, such was the force of the gale.

Turning the bows of the boat back into the wind and sitting side by side pulling on an oar each, we tried desperately to row to the top of the lake, but even pulling on the oars with all our strength, it was impossible to make any impression against the wind and waves. For several minutes we fought the elements to no avail – the boat was being pushed backwards.

Afraid to try anything else, I held the bows into the wind with the oars and allowed the wind to blow us down the lake. The spray was coming in over the bows and hitting my back; my partner was in front of me bailing like mad. By this time waders had been taken off and life jackets put on and checked, as there was a very real possibility that we would have to swim for it. However luck was with us and we were blown from the top of the lake to the bottom, a distance of over one mile in gale force conditions. Arriving at the bottom end of the lake the boat nearly overturned and I jumped out with the mooring rope. The boat, with Arnold holding tight, and me a few metres away pulling hard on the mooring rope was roughly washed up onto the shore. Quickly pulling the boat up to safety and collecting our tackle, we sat back and relaxed. The memory of that incident nearly twenty years ago is as fresh in my mind as if it happened yesterday. It's amazing how a good fright concentrates the mind.

There is only one thing worse than being wet when fishing and that is being cold. When boat fishing on large open waters with no protection from the elements it is important to be dressed warmly. Anglers in North America, owing to the widely diverse nature of their weather, probably on the whole take better precautions than their UK counterparts. Hands and feet are perhaps the most difficult areas to keep warm. Use good quality leather gloves – shooting gloves are good – for the hands and woollen oversocks for the feet. Then you need a thermal vest, moleskin shirt, woollen jumper, body warmer and barbour-type jacket with hood for your upper body; for the lower body, long johns and moleskin trousers. Don't forget to take a thermos flask containing a hot drink of coffee or tea. After the early cold start to the season adjust your clothing according to conditions. Don't get caught out; I have known the wind to come in very cold in May and June on high moorland lakes. Out of the wind in a sheltered spot one can sit without a coat, but in the exposed areas the wind chill factor can be a serious problem.

Another problem the fisherman has to face while fishing is the risk of the lure snagging up on underwater rocks or other obstructions. Even if you know the water well there is always the chance of being caught out. The last flood could have washed down tree trunks or branches right across the lie since you last fished it.

Fear of snagging is why many anglers do not fish their lures effectively. However if it should happen, here are a few tips which may save you from loosing that expensive spinner. If you suddenly snag up don't pull on the line; slack the line off and the spinner may fall out of the snag on its own. If this does not work, gently jerk the rod tip several times to make the spinner rise and fall in the current – this may free it. If this fails, place an otter on the line; this is basically a piece of wood which is attached to the fishing line with a clip. Don't worry if you do not have one, you can soon make one from a piece of branch and nylon line. Let the otter slip down on a tight line, then start giving slack line so the otter floats downstream of the snagged lure, thus forming a belly of line. Hopefully the pull of the otter in the current in a different direction will free the lure. Another dodge which sometimes works is to open the bail arm to put pressure on the line while holding it on the spool with the index finger, then release it suddenly. This will sometimes produce a sufficient backward spring to free the spinner; if necessary repeat the operation a few times.

If all else fails, wrap the line around your forearm over your coat sleeve a few times and pull slowly and directly from the snagged lure as hard as you can without breaking the line, and hold it under pressure. Maintaining this pressure for a time will very often pull it free, or the obstacle or part of it will break away. If all else has failed you will have to break the line and this is sometimes the price we must all pay if we are to fish with efficiency. To avoid leaving metres of line in the water it is good fishing practice to use a smaller breaking strain trace from swivel to lure than the main fishing line so that, in the event of having to break off, the fishing line left behind is of little or no danger generally to wildlife.

# 3

# Plugs and Wobblers

Plugs and wobblers are primary trolling and deep water lures, but there is no doubt they can be, and are, used for all types of fish and waters. There would appear to be two lines of thought on plug and wobbler design.

There is the 'exact imitation' school of thought, where the lure is a realistic copy of the real minnow. The other is the gaudy, bright attractor type of lure that looks like nothing natural but is very effective in provoking fish to strike. My personal view is between the two and I would select my lure depending on the species of fish, time of year and type of water I was fishing.

The exact imitation type of lure probably has the edge when attracting fishermen and we all know when a particular lure or fly becomes popular, everybody rushes out to buy the ultimate fish catcher. This in turn leads to many fishermen catching plenty of fish on the same type of lure resulting in a lot of publicity in the angling press.

Most plugs and wobblers are constructed out of wood or metal. Their basic design ensures that when they are 'fished' through the water movement is imparted to them. How realistic and effective this movement is depends entirely on their design, manufacture and testing.

## Rapala (Finland)

The Rapala was developed in the depression years of the thirties. Lauri Rapala, an obscure Finnish fisherman, had for years fished the forest lakes north of Helsinki, struggling to make a living in the harsh conditions prevailing. During the summer months in his row boat he fished for days, supplementing his nets with lines of baited hooks. Sometimes he had good catches, at other times, nothing. Over the years he studied the bait fish and their predators, observing shoals of minnows as they foraged past and how they behaved when hungry predators launch their forays from the deeper water. With the experience he gained over the years he found he could predict which minnow would be the victim when the shoals were attacked by the predators – mainly trout and northern pike.

Invariably the victim of the predator would be the weakest member of the shoal, usually with some sort of defect in their swimming pattern. The normal attacking method of a predator into a shoal of prey fish is to slash and snap at many individuals as possible on its first run, and then return on the second run and mop up the dead and injured minnows. Some of these injured fish survive and recover, only to become victims at a later date.

Lauri was well aware of this fact and in the summer fishing period of 1936 he developed his idea of a floating lure with a unique twisting movement that would imitate the swimming pattern of an injured or sick minnow. He carved this lure out of pine bark and after a great deal of experimenting with his pine bark wobblers, although they did not look too special, he found he could make them move in a most lifelike and attractive manner. Finding the right design to produce the correct swimming action for the lure was much more difficult. The river near his home became his test-tank and by changing the design slightly after testing each prototype he slowly 'tuned' his lure so that it behaved just like the real thing.

Fishing on Lake Paijanne his catch grew, and soon attracted the attention of his fellow fishermen and he sold them a few lures. All this came to an end in 1939 when the Russians invaded Finland and Lauri joined the army to defend his country.

Three years or so after the war Rapala left his normal work of fisherman and lumberman and in 1949 started to make his lures professionally with help from his family. The demand for the lures grew steadily. The production method was primitive and slow and each lure had to be tested and tuned to Rapala's specifications. Some of the lures found their way across to North America and the demand multiplied. To meet this demand, a new process had to be implemented on a large scale. This meant moving what was basically a cottage industry into a factory environment, without any loss in quality. Production still included the testing and tuning of lures in the water tank, an expensive, time-consuming process. However Rapala decided not to cut corners by leaving this process out, even to meet the very heavy demand for their lures in those early days.

Lauri Rapala died in 1974 at the age of 68 and since then his sons have developed the business and modernized their methods of producing Rapala wobblers. No longer are the wobblers carved by hand. The body is turned out on a lathe from specially selected wood and a steel wire frame is fitted to it. This steel wire joins the hook rings and nose ring to form the basic assembly of the lure. This is coated either with plastic paint or by gluing metal foil onto the body. The next stage is painting the most sophisticated colour combinations. Finally the wobbler is tank tested and adjusted to produce its unique swimming action. At present the Rapala selection consist of thirteen wobbler models with different characteristics and many colour combinations. In this chapter I will only deal with the models intended primarily for fresh water fishing.

## Colour Code Guide for all Rapala Models

| | | | | |
|---|---|---|---|---|
| S | – Silver | | CHB | – Chrome Blue |
| G | – Gold | | GB | – Gold Black |
| B | – Blue | | CW | – Crowdad |
| GFR | – Gold Fluorescent Red | | FT | – Firetiger |
| P | – Perch | | SD | – Shad |
| RT | – Rainbow Trout | | RH | – Redhead |
| SFC | – Silver Fluorescent Chartreuse | | SM | – Silver Mackerel |
| CH | – Chrome | | GM | – Green Mackerel |

## The Original Floating Rapala

| Model | Body Length | Weight |
|---|---|---|
| 5 | 5 cm | 3 g |
| 7 | 7 cm | 4 g |
| 9 | 9 cm | 5 g |
| 11 | 11 cm | 6 g |
| 13 | 13 cm | 7 g |
| 18 | 18 cm | 21 g |

*Colours:* S, G, B, GFR, P, RT

**Husky**

| Model | Body Length | Weight |
|-------|-------------|--------|
| H – 13 | 13 cm | 11 g |

*Colours:* S, SD, B, GFR, P, CW, SFC

**Countdown (Sinking) Rapala**

| Model | Body Length | Weight |
|-------|-------------|--------|
| CD – 5 | 5 cm | 5 g |
| CD – 7 | 7 cm | 8 g |
| CD – 9 | 9 cm | 11 g |
| CD – 11 | 11 cm | 16 g |

*Colours:* S, G, B, GFR, P, RT, SFC

The Floating, Husky and Countdown (Sinking) Rapala are most effective in the following sizes for the following species of fish.

| | |
|---|---|
| Perch: | Models 5 and 7 |
| Trout (all species): | Models 5, 7, 9 and 11 |
| Salmon (all species): | Models 9, 11 and 13 |
| Zander: | Models 7, 9, 11, 13 and 18 |
| Pike: | Models 9, 11, 13 and 18 |
| Chub: | Models 5, 7 and 9 |
| Walleye: | Models 7, 9, 11 and 13 |
| Bass (large and smallmouth): | Models 5, 7, 9, 11 and 13 |

The wobblers model sizes are only given as a general guide, there are bound to be some exceptions.

On lakes the Floating and Husky Rapalas are great performers for the various species of trout. When trolling it pays to slowly let out your Rapala from the boat, watching it carefully as you give it line to ensure it is working properly. If you wish to fish a little deeper, add the required weight to your line to achieve the desired depth. Too much weight on your line is not good for the action of the Floating Rapala; it is far better to change to a countdown model of the same size and colour as your floater. To ensure a Floating Rapala performs well and gives the correct action it is best to tie it on the line with the loop or Rapala knot. Having the lure secured to the line by hanging it in a loop gives it unfettered movement and it performs well – exactly like a crippled minnow trying to escape.

Fishing the shallows from the lakeside really allows your Husky and Floating Rapalas to show their paces. Use as light a fishing line as you dare and attach the line to it with a loop knot. Cast the lure out to a likely looking spot; allow it to settle sub surface. When the disturbance has subsided, retrieve it slowly, running the lure just under the water, allowing it to bulge the surface without actually breaking it. Another useful tactic is to cast out and allow the lure to settle. Now twitch the lure a few times, causing it to quiver and roll. Do this a few times, retrieving the lure a couple of metres between the pauses; then fish the lure in. Very exciting fishing can be had doing this – the takes come from no-where.

For fishing very windy conditions on large areas of water in exposed situations, the Husky 13 makes casting and observation of the lure in a big wave much easier. For deeper fishing add some weight to the fishing line or change to the sinking version of your floater.

The Countdown (Sinking) Rapala is slightly thicker and more rounded in the body and weighted for controlled sinking. This makes it easier to cast into the wind and hold at a pre-determined depth while trolling. It has proved to be an exceptional lure when trolling in lakes, particularly for salmon (all species) and trout (all species). Several very large brown trout of over twenty pounds have been taken this way. The Sinking Rapala is a firm favourite for fishing the shoreline, both on the bank and in the boat. A variation from the normal method of retrieving after casting the lure well out, is to wind it back quickly and then suddenly stop. The lure will flutter as it sinks, any fish that has been following but not taking will be provoked into striking. Do not stop for more than a couple of seconds then continue to retrieve. Always pause before lifting the lure (this applies to any lure) out of the water after fishing out the cast – very often the take will just materalize. It always gives me quite a start when this happens; no matter how prepared I am it is always a surprise.

**The Jointed Rapala**

| Model | Body Length | Weight |
|---|---|---|
| J 7 | 7 cm | 4 g |
| J 9 | 9 cm | 7 g |
| J 11 | 11 cm | 9 g |
| J 13 | 13 cm | 18 g |

*Colours:* S, G, B, GFR, P, SFC

The Jointed Rapala or rather the articulated lure is a natural step up to increase the effectiveness of the lure in certain conditions. It imparts more 'life' to the lure while it is being fished very slowly, extra wiggle on the fore-and-aft axis and a general quiver throughout the entire lure; the whole effect makes it very attractive to hungry predators. It duplicates the distress signal of an injured or crippled minnow exactly. Fishing the articulated lure too fast in still water will decrease rather than increase the effectiveness of the lure at most times. The exception to this is when using it in fast flowing rivers; the very quick action of an articulated lure while being hung over a salmon lie will very often bring the salmon up to strike at the lure. For stillwaters, attach your Jointed Rapala to the line with the loop knot, for rivers the clinch or half-blood knot will do.

The Jointed Rapalas are most effective in the following sizes:

| | |
|---|---|
| Perch: | Model 7 |
| Black Bass: | Models 7, 9, 11 |
| Zander: | Models 7, 9, 11 and 13 |
| Pike: | Models 9, 11 and 13 |
| Trout (all species): | Models 7 and 9 |
| Salmon (all species): | Models 7, 9, 11 and 13 |
| Chub: | Models 7 and 9 |

In cold weather add weight on the line to enable presentation of the lure to the fish which has gone deep. When fishing from the shore, bumping the bottom will often give good results. Don't have the weight any closer that 60 cm (2 ft) to the lure.

**Fat Rap Deep Runner**

| Model | Body Length | Weight |
|---|---|---|
| FR 5 | 5 cm | 11 g |
| FR 7 | 7 cm | 14 g |

**Fat Rap Shallow Runner**

| Model | Body Length | Weight |
|-------|-------------|--------|
| SFR 5 | 5 cm | 8 g |
| SFR 7 | 7 cm | 13 g |

**Mini Fat Rap**

| Model | Body Length | Weight |
|-------|-------------|--------|
| MFR 3 | 3 cm | 4 g |

Colours: S, G, GFR, P, CW, SFC

The Fat Rap was designed for the fisherman who works rod and reel and requires a lure that does the correct thing, that is, on the retrieve it comes back straight and true, not being thrown off course by underwater snags which would cause it to broach, turn on its side or perform some other wild movement; also it recovers quickly from any underwater collision with rocks and weeds or any other submerged objects which would upset its swimming action and result in a wasted cast by the angler.

The original deep running Fat Rap was designed to take fish from mid-water. It is a floating lure and when the angler starts retrieving after a cast, its extra long vane will cause it to dive deeply and the long plastic vane will play it off most snags and weed beds. Any pause in the retrieve will (because of the balsa wood construction) always allow the Fat Rap to float upwards. Remember, the faster the recovery of the line, the more steeply the lure will dive. Experienced anglers will start fishing slowly until the lure bumps the lake bed; they will pause to allow the lure to rise and then repeat the process. Many times the takes will come as the lure floats upwards from these pauses in the retrieve. This can be useful sometimes after a hang-up in the bottom; a short pause, and the lure floats clear of the obstruction, then carry on fishing. The deep-diving Fat Rap comes complete with a split ring attachment and the lure can be tied on the fishing line with a clinch knot.

The Fat Raps are most effective in the following sizes.

| | |
|-------|-------------|
| Perch: | Model 3 |
| Black Bass: | Models 5 and 7 |
| Pike: | Model 7 |
| Trout (all species): | Models 3 and 5 |
| Salmon (all species): | Models 7 and 9 |

The next plug in the Rapala stable is the Shad Rap. This lure is popular in the southern part of the North America and it is available in the following specifications and colours.

**Shad Rap Deep Runner**

| Model | Body Length | Weight |
|-------|-------------|--------|
| SR 5 | 5 cm | 8 g |
| SR 7 | 7 cm | 9 g |
| SR 9 | 9 cm | 15 g |

## Shad Rap Shallow Runner

| Model | Body Length | Weight |
|---|---|---|
| SSR 5 | 5 cm | 6 g |
| SSR 7 | 7 cm | 7 g |
| SSR 9 | 9 cm | 12 g |

*Colours:* S, SD, P, CW, SFC.

Most effective for the following species:

| | |
|---|---|
| Perch: | Model 5 |
| Black Bass: | Models 5, 7 and 9 |
| Walleye: | Models 5, 7 and 9 |
| Trout: | Models 5 and 7 |
| Pike: | Models 7 and 9 |
| Chub: | Models 5 and 7 |
| Salmon: | Models 7 and 9 |

The Shad Rap has proved itself to be very effective with bass, walleye and pike. This lure, because of its superb balance, shows the same swimming characteristics whether it is being retrieved very slowly or superfast. Its action at both ends of the spectrum is equally lifelike: good movement at slow speed and no broaching or wild leaping and twisting at fast speeds. According to the speed of the retrieve the lure will run at a constant depth. For trolling deep, you will need to experiment with various weights until the required depth is achieved. The extra weight should be placed not closer to the lure than 60 cm (2 ft), any closer will impede its action. It is also recommended that the Shad Rap should be fished with a relatively light line; this makes casting easier and allows the lure to swim more naturally.

## Magnum – Sinking

| Model | Length | Weight |
|---|---|---|
| CD 7 Mag | 7 cm | 12 g |
| CD 9 Mag | 9 cm | 17 g |
| CD 11 Mag | 11 cm | 24 g |
| CD 14 Mag | 14 cm | 36 g |
| CD 18 Mag | 18 cm | 70 g |

## Magnum – Floating

| Model | Length | Weight |
|---|---|---|
| 11 Mag | 11 cm | 17 g |
| 14 Mag | 14 cm | 28 g |
| 18 Mag | 18 cm | 45 g |

*Magnum Colours:* S, GFR, GM, RH, SFC.

## Sliver Sinking – Jointed

| Model | Length | Weight |
|---|---|---|
| SL 13 | 13 cm | 18 g |
| SL 20 | 20 cm | 38 g |

*Colours:* S, GFR, GR, RH, NF, SPC.

The Magnum and Sliver are useful for pike and salmon; they are also used for sea fishing.

## Rattl'n Rap

Plugs with an in-built sonic vibrator have been with us for many years. However in 1985 Rapala, in conjunction with American experts, started their quest to develop a new lure using sound as enticement. In the beginning the prototype was tested on bass. The general effectiveness of this lure proved itself on its very first fishing trial in February 1986 on Lake Okeechobee, Florida when the test team in their boat took over one hundred bass – while the other boat teams only caught a few on their spinners.

The hard work involved in developing a lure which presented a perfectly sculptured fish-like body from head to tail with a triple frequency sonic call was soon to bring its rewards. The lure consists of two chambers; in the first chamber are three metal balls – in the second, the rear chamber, there are ten metal balls. The balls in the front chamber and the balls in the rear chamber transmit high and medium frequency sounds; low sounds are also produced by the swimming action of the Rattl'n Rap. The triple combination of low, medium and high frequency sounds in this lure produce a rhythmic call that the fish are alerted to, as they are able to pick up a wide range of sounds; they pick up the low frequencies beyond the range of human hearing by their lateral line organ. Hydrophone tests established that the Rattl'n Rap treble frequency call has a range of twelve metres or more. It is extremely effective and more harmonic and rhythmic than most sonic lures.

### Rattl'n Rap

| Model | Length | Weight |
|-------|--------|--------|
| RNR 5 | 5 cm | 7 g |
| RNR 7 | 7 cm | 14 g |

*Colours:* CH, CHB, GB, CW, FT, SD.

The next model planned is the RNR 8; this model will contain three large balls in front and twelve small balls in the rear chamber. These lures are recommended for bass, pike, zander and trout in fresh water, and are also useful for saltwater fishing.

**Tuning**   It is extremely important that your wobbler is fishing properly. Lures take a lot of knocks in a day's fishing including collisions or hang-ups with underwater obstructions or a mammoth battle with a gigantic fish. When your Rapala is not fishing as it should, look for the following symptoms. The lure does not track true; it will broach or makes wild movements and generally not give the action for which it was designed. When you have a lure behaving in this fashion, it will need to be adjusted (tuned) to fish in the manner as designed.

The first thing to do is to sight along its bottom axis from the eye ring towards the tail. If any of the treble hooks are hanging off-centre, this indicates a displaced hook hanger. Take a pair of finely pointed pliers and gently bend the hanger back towards the centre line of the lure, so all the triangles are hanging in a row. Always check the tail ring hanger as the tail always receives rough treatment, being hit and hooking fish. Experienced anglers will always check that the hooks are in line; it is good fishing practice to give your lure a visual sighting every so often, even if you have not caught anything. Give the triangles frequent inspection to ensure the hook points are still needle sharp.

If the lure is not running true on retrieve, veering from one side to the other, the most probable cause is that the eye hanger is out of line. If your Rapala veers to the right, use your pliers carefully to bend the eye-hanger to the left, a little at a time, until the fault is corrected. Use the same technique in reverse if the lure should veer to the left.

Rapalas are produced in a modern factory in Vaaksy, Finland, employing a

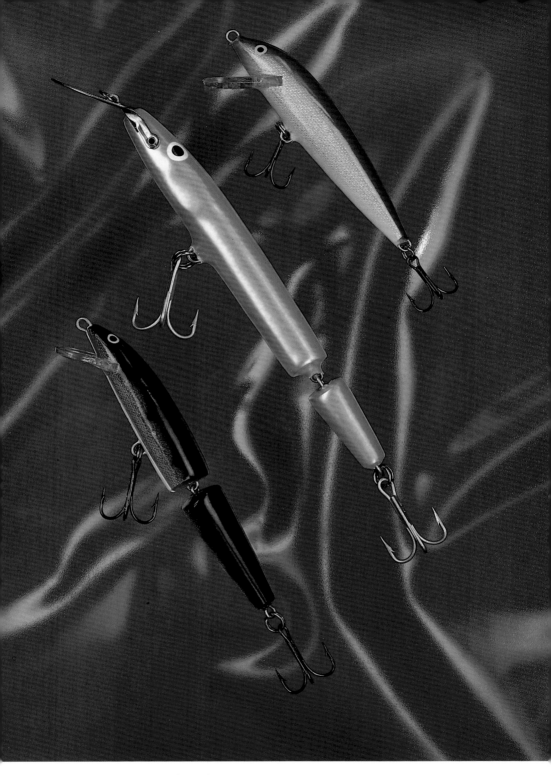

*Plate 1*   Rapala (*from the top*): Countdown; Silver-Jointed; Jointed.
*Photo: Gordon Bellman*

*Plate 2* Rapala (*from the top*): Floating; Rattl'n Rap; Fat Rap; Shad Rap.
*Photo Gordon Bellman*

great many people; they also employ local housewives working skilfully and carefully in their own homes. Rapala has now joined with the Normark Corporation, USA, to form one of the largest tackle groups on the international scene.

At the time of writing it is fifty-four years since Lauri Rapala carved his first pine bark minnow to catch fish to earn money so as to enable him to buy the basic requirements for his family. I wonder if in his wildest dreams he thought that he was designing a product that would give his children and their children the security he had never known in his young adult life.

## Shakespeare Company UK (Ltd)

The next selection of plugs are from the Shakespeare stable – starting with the Big S which is a great favourite with the pike angler.

**Big S**   length 90 mm, weight 20 g. It is available in a wide range of colours and is an extremely effective plug for pike. It is very well designed and looks like a small bream. Its finish is faultless, the treble hooks are good quality and the split rings hold the hooks well clear of the lure body, which should stop any levering by the fish.

The Big S has two stable mates, Medium and Small S, which are available in the same colours and have the same good finish. These plugs are extremely successful for taking pike, perch, zander and chub. Although they are floating lures they can be fished deep on a paternoster. Tie the weight on a breakaway point about 60 cm (2 ft) long. Fish the plug with the weight bumping the lake's bottom. The lure, because of its natural buoyancy, will fish about 30 cm or so (1 ft) off the bottom. Using the sink and draw method can be successful on the paternoster as by casting out and letting the weight rest on the bottom, the buoyant Big S will slowly rise. Retrieve it slowly with an erratic sink and draw action. It is easy, in the event of snagging, to allow the plug to float clear and if necessary break off the weight and recover the lure.

For successful pike fishing the way the swim is approached is critical. The approach must be slow and careful, taking full advantage of any bankside cover. Stop a few metres short of the bank; try a few short casts into the water immediately in front, as if a bait-feeding bottom angler has been fishing and feeding the swim before you, there is always a chance that the pike have followed the prey fish in close to the bank. If there is nothing doing, move cautiously to the edge of the bank still using what cover there is. Now start searching the whole area with short casts, left and right, gradually fanning them out to cover the whole swim. If you suspect a pike has touched or followed the lure in, and on the next cast if nothing has happened, give that part of the swim a rest for a while. Perhaps changing the size of your plug, up or down depending on the size the pike first showed interest in, will provoke it.

There is no set pattern for fishing a swim. Some people fish it systematically, others use their experience of the water and fish accordingly. On strange water it is perhaps best to fish the likely stretches systematically. Often, when fishing the plug just under the surface fairly quickly, you become aware of the bow wave of a following fish. I always find this very exciting fishing and it is difficult to decide whether to speed the lure up or to slow it down. Remember, depending on the size of the fish it could be anywhere from 30 cm up to a metre or so ahead of the actual bow wave you see.

Give a plug a good trial before changing, there is nothing to be gained by changing the lure every few casts. You will find your concentration is not what it should be and you could end up fishing badly, even perhaps miss hooking the only strike of the day.

One of the worst faults of anglers, generally inexperienced fishermen, is that when spinning for pike they fish too fast and shallow. Plugs, I know, are expensive and being careful not to snag up and lose them is understandable. Beginners would increase their chances by fishing a little more slowly if not deeply. Bear in mind the pike prefer plugs some days rather more so than spoons and bar-spinners. The beginner will soon realise the chances of losing plugs is much less than the metal spinners.


## Abu Garcia Limited (UK)

This company manufacture a comprehensive selection of plugs which in my view would be adequate for whatever application the angler chooses. They are effective for the following species of fish: pike, zander, perch, trout, salmon, bass and the chub.

**Killer Balsa Sinking**   Available in three sizes, weight 7, 12, and 18 g. Colours: silver, blue gill, green, orange fluorescent, and the yellow fluorescent.

**Killer Balsa Floating**   Two sizes: 6 and 9 g. Good quality balsa wood lures. Both the floating and sinking versions have good colour combinations and are well finished. Should swim well in any water conditions.

**Killer Balsa Magum**   A really hefty sized lure, available in two sizes: 140 mm/40 g and 180 mm/73 g making it an excellent lure for salmon and large lake pike. It is a good trolling plug and performs well for the saltwater species. Colours: redhead, bluegill, fluorescent orange and fluorescent yellow.

**Killer Shad Floating**   Useful all-round lure for both lake and river. Available in one size only. Colours: silver, bluegill, green, fluorescent yellow and fluorescent orange. A proven master of those deep steamy runs and dark pools in rivers; a specially designed front vane gives it excellent diving capabilities and its appealing action makes it an extremely effective lure for most species of fish.

**Morrum Jig**   Effective all-rounder, three sizes 38 mm/7 g, 40 mm/10 g and 50 mm/20 g. Only colour: fluorescent orange. The Morrum Jig, to be effective, needs to be retrieved at varying speeds with a jerky action. The head is constructed of solid metal which causes the lure to dive head first, and a fast jerky retrieve will give it an erratic action while being fished – at times this can be quite effective. Its design makes casting in tricky conditions against the wind much easier.

**Hi Lo Sinking**   Two sizes, 80 mm/18 g and 65 mm/12 g.

**Hi Lo Floating**   Two sizes, 110 mm/26 g and 150 mm/40 g.

**Hi Lo Jointed Sinking** 90 mm/20 g. Hi Lo colours: pike scale, red head, bluegill, perch scale and fluorescent orange.

All diving vanes on the Hi Lo plugs are adjustable to six different settings, allowing six diving settings from shallow to very deep angles. The articulated version is an appealing mover giving an extremely realistic swimming effect. In turbulent water conditions, big waves or swift flowing currents, or by knocking itself into under-water weedbeds or other obstructions, it is not unknown for the diving vane to alter its setting. It is important therefore to check the vane and hooks frequently, thus ensuring the lure is fishing as intended.

## Lindquist Bros Bait Co Ltd (Canada): Canadian Wigglers

The Wiggler story started about fifty years ago in Canada when Walter Lindquist Snr, originally from Finland, started experimenting with various materials for making lures. Apart from his family his great passion in life was fishing.

During the summer months, after finishing work for the day at the local car factory where he was wheel production foreman, he would take himself off to the well stocked Lake St Clair, which was near his home on the outskirts of Windsor, Ontario.

It was here that he developed his fishing lures to use on the residents of Lake St Clair: bass, muskie, walleye and pike. A half-hour fishing and rowing around in his boat was all that was needed for him to forget the humdrum of working eight hours a day in a busy machine shop. During the winter months he worked on his lures, improving on the lessons learned during his fishing trips.

Finally at the age of fifty-three when most of us are looking to take life a little easier and starting to think of retirement, he gave notice after working for the same company for twenty-eight years. His wife had some misgivings about his decision; she liked the idea of a regular weekly wage coming in. However, he took the step in 1949, confident in his ability to make a living using his fully equipped basement workshop. Together with his sons, Arnold and Walter Jnr and their wives, the initial production run of Canadian Wigglers was set in motion.

The Lindquists were determined to produce a quality product and to this end no effort was spared and this is still true today. There are several stages of production: first a blanking and forming machine cuts and shapes the brass metal into the well-known Wiggler shape; next is the trimming and curling process; finally the seams are welded, and then buffed to a smooth finish. After the tumbling and cleaning takes place, the product begins to take on a fish-catching look. The next stage is the colour combination: first the lure is painted with its primer, followed by its base coat; now the colour design is sprayed and hand painted on, followed by a lacquer finish to complete the Wiggler.

The Wiggler is now tested for its swimming ability by being pulled through the test tank. If the swimming action is not up to the high standard required, it is back to the workshop. Every lure is so finely designed that any out of alignment of the eye ring will destroy the action and the effectiveness of the Wiggler is reduced.

Walter Lindquist Jnr makes the point that the Canadian Wiggler is designed to fish through the water at any depth; unlike most other lures it is made from brass tubing – therefore is practically indestructable. The brass body gives it the weight for deep trolling as well as the strength to endure the most vigorous movement.

The eye rings are actually welded into the brass as opposed to being screwed in as is done with plastic or wood. Walter makes the point: 'We never have had problems with the eyes being ripped out in a battle with a big one. If it did happen, I would be more than happy to replace the lure with a new one.'

Walter Lindquist Snr passed away in 1985 but the business continues to be operated by his sons, Walter Jnr and Arnold, producing for the fishermen of the world eight models and over fifty colours of the Canadian Wiggler. There is virtually a model type and colour of Canadian Wiggler for any freshwater predator and probably many of the saltwater predators as well. Models available are: MJ-Jointed Trolling; M-Trolling; CWJ-Jointed Casting & Trolling; CW-Casting & Trolling; S-Spinning; J-Spinning; SF-Spinning & Floater; CWR-Casting & Trolling Rattler.

The Wiggler will take the full range of game fish and the major predators such as pike, zander and perch. They gained some notoriety for their ability taking Coho, Kokanee and Chinook salmon in the great lakes of the North America. Arnold Lindquist recommends the fluorescent colours; according to him the 'hot ones' for trout, salmon and walleye are Wiggler Models CW 28, CW 2 and CW 6. Many of the charter boat captains in all waters of the Great Lakes system troll with good effect, using the Wiggler for salmon, trout and pickeral.

Trolling in the UK for salmon and trout with the Wiggler has been quite successful. Probably the best sizes for fishing the rivers in the UK are CW and CWJ for salmon with the Model S for sea trout. For pike or zander Models CW and CWJ would be most suitable. Chub and perch would probably come to Models S or J.

Weight is not normally needed on the line to make the Wiggler fish deep. The faster the lure is retrieved the deeper they will fish. In high water conditions when it is necessary to fish slow and deep it may be better to add a little weight on the fishing line.

Wigglers have proved to be remarkably effective on Scottish waters for salmon and trout and they are, I believe, doing well in Ireland. There is quite an art fishing the Wiggler in fast-flowing small rocky spate rivers. When using the lure it is necessary to develop a feel, or rather a feeling technique if you are to make it fish properly. In the fast rocky runs it will pay to fish the Wiggler like a salmon fly. Let the current take it after a cast but ensure it is kept on a tight line, do not let it bury itself in the river bed. As the Wiggler comes around on a tight line, you will feel the vibration of the lure working. When the lure is downstream of you, it is time to start the retrieve. Bring the Wiggler back slowly – allow the flow of the water to impart life, movement and vibration to it.

Over forty years (at the time of writing) has passed since the Canadian Wiggler first saw the light of day and started taking fish. It is now known worldwide. It has been many years since the production of the Wiggler outgrew the basement workshop and moved to the new factory in Windsor. Many of the employees who started with Lindquist in the early days of business are still there; most have over fifteen years of service, a couple have been there for over thirty years – performing the same work to provide for the current generation of fishermen the same Wigglers as they did for their fathers. Now a grandson has joined the business and is employed at the factory, thus carrying on the family business of supplying fishing lures to the fishermen of the world to the next generation.

## Tomic Lures (Canada)

Tom Moss has been actively involved with fishing all his life. Born and raised in Victoria, on Vancouver Island, British Columbia, he was introduced to the great outdoor environment at an early age. Tom acquired a solid grounding in salt-water fishing on the salmon rich west coast waters of British Columbia, with freshwater experience gained by fishing the lakes and rivers of Vancouver Island.

Such was his introduction into the commercial fishing environment that by the time of his eighteenth birthday he was a successful professional fishing guide. It was during the early years of being a fishing guide that he began to realise the shortcomings of many of the commercial lures. To overcome the design faults of some of these he modified them to meet his understanding of what was needed for local marine conditions.

His modified plugs were proving so successful that in 1961 he started designing and producing his own experimental prototypes. In 1962, he set up production in an old chicken shed. His first year's production was 4,000 three inch (75 mm) Tomic Lures, which were selling as fast as he could produce them. Seven years later the demand was so great that to increase production he had to move to larger premises and he moved his production unit to new facilities located at the entrance of Sooke harbour, a west coast fishing port.

It is the wide range of colour designs – over five hundred Tomic colours – which makes it possible for the angler to select the correct lure to match whatever conditions are prevailing. Key factors that influence the choice of colour are the time of year and natural foods available.

Tom's charters would catch fifty to sixty fish a day, with his best day being ninety chinooks. The success Tom was having with his three inch (75 mm) Tomic plug was noticed by the commercial fishermen and they approached him to develop a larger plug, which he did – the seven inch (180 mm) Tomic. The interest coming from the commercial people resulted in more extensive research and development. Today ninety per cent of the trolling fleets from Alaska to Californa make use of Tomic plugs during the season.

Newly created designs take a couple of years before they go into production. Tomic lures are constructed from hollow plastic blanks which are in two sections, head (front section) and tail (rear section). The liner, which may be of brass or silver, is placed into the hollow plastic blank. After inserting the liner, the head and tail are glued together. All plugs are hand cleaned to remove excess glue and to ensure a smooth joint which is important for the plug's action. The whole plug is now dipped in acetone, returning it to a full finish. This treatment also cleans it in preparation for painting.

The five hundred plus Tomic colour designs are painted by airbrush artists, some of the designs requiring up to twelve colours before they are completed.

**Tomic 'Multi' Lure**   It took three years to develop the 'Multi' which is now available in most colours and two sizes, three inch (75 mm) and seven inch (180 mm). It is rigged with two treble hooks that will not tangle when the plug is cast, popped or trolled. Rattles are available on request, but not required for the chrome models – 900 series.

The Multi is a balanced floating plug designed to create an erratic swimming pattern when fished at slow or fast speeds in deep or shallow water. Included in the colours available for the Multi is a phosphorous-based plastic plug that provides a long-lasting rechargeable glow. Species of fish taken by the Multi plug include: bass, salmon all species, trout all species, pike and many saltwater predators.

**Tomic 'Classic' Lure**     Five sizes, ranging from three inches (75 mm) to seven inches (180 mm) and over sixty colours are available for the original Tomic design. Classic plugs have been for the last twenty-five years used by the west coast commercial troll fleets. Made from Butyrate, a tough lightweight plastic, it is now available for the serious sports angler. Besides being trolled it can be cast and fished from shore and bank, lake or river. It is extremely effective when fished with a rod and line spinning outfit for all predators.

**Tomic Broken-Back**     Drawing on his thirty-five years of fishing experience, Tom Moss designed his unique jointed plug. Its balanced design allows the tail to move independently of the head, at the same time allowing the plug to maintain the traditional action of the Classic, which imitates the swimming pattern of an injured or crippled bait fish in a realistic manner.

Broken-Backs are rigged with two treble hooks – one on the tail and one under the head. The head and tail sections are joined together with brass nickel-plated eyelets that are actually moulded into the plastic for extra strength. Tom Moss has designed this lure to withstand the rigours of commercial fishing conditions, taking strike after strike without the fear of losing fish. It is versatile enough to be cast without the hooks becoming entangled and it can be fished at high or low speeds, in fast flowing rivers or still-waters.

Available in over sixty colours, it lures a wide variety of fish including salmon, trout, pike and the various predators that are to be found in waters around the world. Since being imported into the United Kingdom, the Classic has proved to be extremely effective. On many Scottish waters it has often outfished the more traditional lures.

It is impossible to list all the colours for the various Tomic lures from the vast selection available. However, there will be plenty of scope for the serious sport fisherman to find a lure to meet his specific fishing requirement in regard to colour. According to Donald Glass of Fife, Scotland, the most popular colours for the Classic in British waters are: silver/chartreuse, silver/blue, gold/orange, gold/orange scale, black/blue, chartreuse, chartreuse/gold scale, pearl/pink stripe, pearl, olive/gold scale, chartreuse fire dot.

The first time I used the Classic I was impressed by the beautiful fish-appealing swimming action this lure has. I was fishing a small fast rocky spate river which usually, when trying to fish deep, results in the loss of tackle. The Classic handled the conditions beautifully; when being retrieved across the current the lure came wobbling across the river deep down in the water under full control. Another characteristic of this lure that I liked – as I do in any other floating plug – is that after casting out the plug, you let it float with the current until you judge the position is correct and then start the retrieve, which will cause the plug to dive and make it possible to present the lure correctly across the salmon lie. This is a good technique for covering the known lies; also these plugs are easy to hang over the lies with their fish-appealing swimming action.

Classic's have only the single treble hook under the belly, attached to the hook holder with a split ring. If you wish, you can add a small code X3 Partridge flying treble hook on a piece of nylon line to the belly hook holder, so that it fishes just below the lure's tail. Do not have the nylon line longer than the lure or there will be some problems with the flying treble catching up on the fishing line or hookholder and sometimes the eye ring. To stop this from happening, place a rubber band over the lure body, holding the flying treble underneath like a tail treble hook. When a fish hits it and becomes hooked, the rubber band will slide up the body or break off. The thinner the rubber band, the better it is for the swimming action of the lure.

# 4

# Homemade Spinners

I became interested in tackle making by pure accident. Although I am an experienced fly-dresser and the bulk of my angling is fly-fishing for game fish, I do have a very wide interest in all types of methods and species, even a limited amount of sea-fishing experience. Most of my local rivers do not suit fly-fishing because they are heavily wooded and in some cases the terrain on the banks is so difficult the only way to cover the water is by spinning or bait fishing.

My interest in spinner design started after I had a particularly difficult day's fishing with a bar-spinner. Fish after fish hit the spinner only to come off a couple of seconds later. I just could not understand what was going wrong. The fish felt as though they were well hooked until a couple of splashy jumps later – then off they came. That evening I decided to attach another treble hook in tandem to the original, but the end result looked rather fearsome. To cover this up and to make it more attractive to the fish, I tied up some tandem treble mounts with the leading treble hook dressed with a bucktail wing encircling the hookshank. Thus was born my fly tails for bar-spinners. The fly tail on the standard bar-spinner certainly did improve its efficiency in attracting the fish and gave a very much improved hooking capacity.

To make my fly tail mount is very easy; first take a piece of nylon monofilament of 11 lb (4·99 kg) breaking strain and about 10 inches (25 cm) long; fold this length of nylon line three times, thus making a total breaking strain of 33 lb (14·98 kg). Place a size eight Partridge X3 treble in the fly-tying vice and whip a few turns of brightly coloured silk on the shank. Lay the nylon line on the hookshank and pass it through the legs of the treble and double it back, laying it back against the hookshank. Pull the nylon line tight so that the loop you have made by passing the nylon line through the legs of the treble hook is pulled up tight between the legs. Secure the nylon line to the hookshank by whipping turns of silk over it, thereby forming a brightly-coloured body with the rear treble of the mount. Leaving the six loose ends of nylon line looking out over the hookshank, now finish the whipping with a three turn whip finish. Give the whipping a couple coats of varnish. When the varnish is dry the rear treble hook can be then joined to the front treble hook.

To prepare the leading treble, first place it in the vice and whip on a bed of silk. Take the rear treble and lay the loose nylon ends on the shank of the leading treble and secure them in place with a few turns of silk. Now adjust the distance of the eye of the rear treble to the fork of the legs of the leading treble. Try to keep this as close as possible; the hookeye should be nearly touching the centre of the legs of the leading treble. When the distance has been adjusted, whip the nylon two-thirds down the hookshank leading to the hookeye. Cut off three of the nylon loose ends just in line with the bottom of the hookeye. Pass the other three loose ends through the hookeye, double them back and overtie. After cutting off the surplus ends, varnish the front treble whipping and leave it to dry.

When the varnish on the whippings of the mount is dry, place the front treble hook in the vice and whip on a bed of silk to take the bucktail wing. Take a bunch of hair and tie it on the hookshank, repeating this until the hookshank has been encircled with bucktail. Cut off the surplus hair looking out over the hookeye and form the head. When the head is completed, finish with a three turn whip. Varnish liberally, thereby cementing the hair and silk together to form a secure and durable head. If you wish you can add Flashabou or Lureflash to the hairwing to give it added attraction.

I made up a few mounts with tails of various colours. Enlisting the help of a friend, Chris Martindale, we went to the river to give them a trial. I gave Chris a gold bar-spinner with a light brown bucktail fly tail to try and I tried a hot orange fly tail with a copper bar-spinner. The results were very encouraging, the fish came well to both colours and stayed well hooked, apart from the odd fish which in the first place had not taken the spinner cleanly – just knocking. Since that time, friends have tested over the years many combinations of colours. The dressings of the mounts which follows are the most effective. Hooks for the mounts are: front X1 size six, rear X3 size eight.

## Fly Tail Patterns

**Black/Silver** *Spinner blade*: silver. *Mount*: black bucktail mixed silver Flashabou.

**Copper/Orange** *Spinner blade*: copper. *Mount*: brown and orange bucktail.

**Gold/Yellow** *Spinner blade*: gold. *Mount*: yellow and brown bucktail.

**Gold/Green** *Spinner blade*: gold. *Mount*: dyed green squirrel tail.

**Copper/Brown** *Spinner blade*: copper. *Mount*: brown bucktail.

**Copper/Red** *Spinner blade*: copper. *Mount*: red and brown bucktail.

The above combinations are very good for clear water conditions and are extremely effective when cast upstream and fished back very quickly.

**Silver/Red** *Spinner blade*: silver. *Mount*: red Flashabou.

**Silver/Blue** *Spinner blade*: silver. *Mount*: blue Flashabou.

**Silver/Yellow** *Spinner blade*: silver. *Mount*: yellow bucktail and gold Flashabou.

**Gold/Orange** *Spinner blade*: gold. *Mount*: hot orange bucktail and gold Flashabou.

**Gold/Magenta** *Spinner blade*: gold. *Mount:* Dyed magenta bucktail and copper Flashabou.

**Silver** *Spinner blade*: silver. *Mount*: silver Flashabou.

**Gold** *Spinner blade*: gold. *Mount*: gold Flashabou.

**Copper**   *Spinner Blade*: copper. *Mount:* copper Flashabou.

The above bar-spinners and tails are designed for coloured water and are extremely effective for salmon and sea trout; they are also good for brown and rainbow trout in most waters.

The mount's nylon breaking strain between the two treble hooks, if constructed as instructed and within the breaking strain of the nylon monofilament used, will be most reliable. I have never had any problems or failures and have taken fish up to fourteen pounds (6·35 kg) quite easily. However it must be understood that nylon monofilament, if exposed to ultra-violet rays, will deteriorate over a period of time. It is advisable to check them regularly, particularly after landing several big fish. Carelessness will only lose you fish. These tandem treble hook fly mounts may not be acceptable on some waters, check the rules first.

## Spoons

Spoons are very effective lures but they need good water movement for them to work effectively. In stillwaters the spoon needs to be trolled or retrieved at a reasonable speed for it to produce its best action. In rivers, the faster the current the better the spoon will perform. The fast current (or a fast retrieve in slow water) will cause the spoon to kick over regularly. If a spoon is retrieved slowly in stillwater or slow running water it will spend most of its time on one plane and only kick over occasionally to show its other side. I have found the narrower the width of the spoon, the more likely it is to perform in such a fashion in these types of water. Usually the broader the spoon the better is its action in slower water; the slimmer spoons are usually more suited for the faster flowing waters. To make a spoon kick over regularly in slow water you will need to retrieve at irregular speeds and keep changing its direction. This you will find helps to make it perform more like the real thing.

A good indicator of how the spoon is working is the 'flash' in the water while retrieving. The more flashes you see, the more times the spoon has kicked over. The flashes comes from the belly or underside of the spoon which is normally unpainted. Even with silver or gold spoons, because one side of the spoon is usually a fish scale pattern, the flash can be picked out most times from the smooth side in the water.

Fly tails are effective on spoons; it is best to have single hook mounts only for long spoons. Large spoons, because of their length and mass, offer the hooked fish a lever to slip the hook. In an attempt to reduce these losses I have devised a separate trace. The construction is as same as the Devon minnow mount. For large spoons make the trace including the swivel long enough for the Partridge X1 treble hook to be well clear of the bottom edge of the spoon. Secure the top swivel of the trace to the spoon's top split ring. Have a length of copper wire wrapped from the spoon bottom split ring. Push the loose end of the copper wire through the eye of treble hook and pull it in close to the bottom end of the spoon and then double it back. When a fish takes the spoon the force of the strike will release the treble from the spoon and the fish will have less opportunity of slipping the hook. Spoons are very good attractors of fish but unless the fish has taken it well back in the mouth the losses are high.

I have experimented with traces that have allowed the spoon to run up the line out of harm's way when the fish has been hooked. Although my prototypes have worked well after the fish has taken, I found the action of the spoon had changed. Using traces where the motive power causes the spoon to be pushed through the water rather than being pulled as their designer intended, does change its fishing action. At the moment I am not happy with the fishing action these traces produce and need to do more experimenting before I can feel confident they are producing the results I require.

The easy way to make a tail to adorn the spoon lure is to wind a hackle or tie in a couple of short pieces of wool on the treble hook. This certainly will improve the taking qualities of the lure. Useful colours are yellow, orange, lime green, magenta and white.

## Quill Minnows

These minnows are very effective takers of trout and sea trout where they occur. They are very easy to make and the sizes and colours are the angler's choice. The colours I normally use are brown/yellow, blue/silver, black/gold, green/yellow and natural quill clear varnished.

Using quill minnows in the small sizes for clear water fishing requires a sensitive rod and fine fishing lines, particularly if you are only using the weight of the minnow to make your casts with no additional weight on the fishing line. The ideal tackle for lightweight spinning is a soft action rod of eight to nine feet (2·40 or 2·70 metres) and a fixed-spool reel filled with six pound (2·40 kg) breaking strain line. Fishing with this equipment in some of the overgrown underfished small streams and the upper reaches of some tributaries of game rivers will give the angler some testing fishing. These waters are small, in some instances perhaps no more than a couple of metres in width and not very deep over most of their length, with their banks covered with thick vegetation which has to be carefully negotiated while fishing them. Some of these small streams do not see more than a couple of fishermen a year. For the angler who is able to apply fieldcraft and is fully experienced in handling his tackle, some excellent fishing will be his for the taking.

This type of fishing I always find very stimulating. To be successful means always fishing your way upstream. The banks in most cases are heavily bushed with hazel, willow, alder, thorn and many other species of trees and bushes. Add to this brambles, ferns and a whole host of other tall plant life. If you are the first angler covering that piece for the year, you have to gently and quietly part the vegetation and ease your rod tip out over the water, and make an upstream cast with your lure. On UK waters from mid-June onwards there is always a chance there will be some sea trout about. The upstream cast and fishing the quill minnow back quickly will certainly attract them if your approach has been unobserved. If you are not particularly skilful in handling a rod and line or have an impatient nature this may not be the ideal mode of fishing for you. When casting under low-lying branches, any miscalculation in your cast means instead of your lure being in the water it ends up being wrapped around a small twig or the treble hooks hooked into some vegetation. The disturbance that follows whilst freeing your spinner means that piece of water is unlikely to be productive – although I always fish it afterwards. It is amazing that when pushing one's self slowly and quietly through vegetation to gain access to the water one's rod, reel, line and the vegetation develop minds of their own. If there is a branch or bramble spur pointing up, the fishing line will somehow manage to get itself wrapped around it, or you are pushing your rod top out over the water when this happens. Or perhaps you are in position with the rod tip out over the water and you release the spinner to make an underhand cast; somehow it manages to hook itself on the vegetation just protruding out from the water at your feet.

Rough stream fishing of this type is not for the faint-hearted or the impatient fisher. However if you take your time and enjoy the peace and beauty of your surroundings it is a good way to spend a few hours, you may even catch some fish. I am fortunate to have access to some fishing on a small stream which flows through a wild valley. Normally I do not fish it until the end of June and by that time it is like a jungle; it takes several visits before I can move into the casting points relatively easy.

## Prawn Spinner
Originally I dressed a prawn imitation for fly-fishing. Since then I have developed the following technique for producing a prawn imitation that wobbles and spins.

### Materials
1. Hollow plastic tubing, similar to the type used for car screen washers.
2. Rubber foam, the same as used for furniture padding.
3. Bucktail hair.
4. Gold oval tinsel.
5. Clear plastic for vane.

This prawn is constructed using normal fly-tying methods and tools. Place an eyeless large salmon hook into the fly-tying vice and tighten. This will act as a mount for the plastic tube. Cut a piece of plastic tube 8 cm (3 in) long for the prawn body and push it on to the hookshank. Whip a bed of silk over the complete length of the tube. To enable the prawn to fish the correct way on, add a strip of weight on the side of the tube; this will be the underside of the prawn. The vane is cut from clear plastic; this can be taken from any suitable clear plastic bottle providing it is stiff enough. Cut the vane to shape with a long strip tail which will enable it to be tied onto the tube. To mould the vane to shape, soak it for a few minutes in hot water – after being removed the vane should bend without cracking. Tie in the vane and coat the binding with varnish and allow to dry. After the varnish is dry, cut a narrow strip of foam rubber, tie in and wind, forming the underbody of the prawn. For the feelers, which should also be about 8 cm (3 in) long, tie in bucktail and gold Flashabou mixed, encircling the tube; tie in another strip of foam with a length of gold overall tinsel, wind the foam rubber and rib it with the gold oval tinsel forming a prawn-shaped body. Secure both foam rubber and tinsel and cut off the surplus. Behind the vane, tie in a throat hackle of long cock fibres and finish off with a tidy silk head and whip finish. Foam rubber provides a soft lifelike body which I feel encourages the fish to hold it longer, thus giving more chance of setting the hooks.

The prawn, now approximately 16 cm (6 in) long, should be secured to the fishing line by passing the line through the tube and then a tulip and treble tied on. The tube now settles on the treble hook with the tulip holding it in place, and the bucktail veiling the treble hook. If you are concerned that the movement of the tube will in time cause some fraying of the fishing line at the vane end of the tube, you may prefer to secure the prawn to the fishing line with a Devon minnow type mount. You will find the tube is flexible and by bending it slightly out of alignment you will make it spin faster. The following dressings are the most effective.

**Orange Prawn**
*Body*    Dyed hot orange foam rubber ribbed gold oval
*Feelers*    Dyed hot orange bucktail and gold Flashabou
*Hackle*    Dyed hot orange cock fibres

**Red Prawn**
*Body*    Dyed red foam rubber ribbed gold oval
*Feelers*    Dyed red bucktail and red Flashabou
*Hackle*    Dyed red cock fibres

**Brown Prawn**
*Body*    Dyed yellow foam rubber ribbed gold oval
*Feelers*    Brown bucktail and gold Flashabou
*Hackle*    Brown cock fibres

**Green/Yellow Prawn**
*Body*    Dyed yellow foam rubber ribbed gold oval
*Feelers*    Dyed green bucktail and gold Flashabou
*Hackle*    Dyed green cock fibres

*Hook size*    Partridge X1 or X3 treble six or four.

Before fishing the prawn, dip it in the water and allow the foam to soak it up. This will give it added weight and assist the casting and it may not be necessary to add weight on the line. When fishing the prawn, cast it far enough upstream to allow sinking time to achieve the depth required. Keep a tight line on it and allow it to fish itself around in the current. Salmon will often have a look at it and not take; sometimes the only indication you will get that you have 'turned' a fish is a flash in the water. When this happens rest the fish for a few minutes, then try again. If the same thing happens again or nothing happens, change to a bar-spinner or spoon and cover the fish again. Usually I will change to a bar-spinner with a fly tail the same colour as the prawn's feelers.

## Bar-Tube Spinner

I designed the tube bar-spinner for use on waters where the rules forbid the use of tandem treble hook mounts. This design is quite simple and uses any commercial bar-spinner where the original treble hook has been damaged and needs replacing. Before any of this can be done a mount needs to be constructed to carry the tube fly. Take a piece of stainless steel wire 5 cm (approx. 2 in) long; fashion an eye to take the treble hook. Now slip the ready dressed fly tube on to the steel shaft and bend the wire to form the other eye – this will keep the tube on the mount. With split rings either end, join the tube to the bar-spinner and the treble hook to the tube mount. The bar-spinner and tube fly combination is now complete.

## Bar-spinner Tube Patterns

### Black and Silver
*Spinner blade*   Silver
*Tube*   Silver tinsel ribbed silver oval
*Wing*   Black squirrel with silver Flashabou

### Black and Gold
*Spinner blade*   Gold
*Tube*   Gold tinsel ribbed gold oval
*Wing*   Black squirrel with gold Flashabou

### Green and Copper
*Spinner blade*   Copper
*Tube*   Copper tinsel ribbed gold oval
*Wing*   Dyed green calf

### Brown and Gold
*Spinner blade*   Copper
*Tube*   Gold tinsel ribbed gold oval
*Wing*   Brown squirrel

This bar-spinner tube fly combination has proved to be very effective in most water conditions and for all species of predatory fish in fresh water. It is extremely good for daytime fishing for the very wary sea trout. Many years ago on one afternoon in August I fished the pools on my local river in low-water conditions with the Brown and Gold tube spinner for the first time. The results were quite unbelievable: the first two casts produced two sea trout; the next three casts, fish chased the spinner but turned away at the last moment, probably seeing me because of the lack of cover. It is very difficult to conceal oneself on a river bed which has become exposed because of the drought. I only fished forty metres of river bank that afternoon and had five fish in the creel, which is a very good result when you consider conditions should have been impossible and I only went to test-swim my experimental design.

Colour combinations for this design are endless; for dirty water conditions tubes dressed with blue or red Flashabou are extremely good; it does not quite matter so much what colour the spinner blade is. For salmon fishing I have increased the length of the tubes and their mounts. Some of my tubes have been 10 cm (4 in) long; add to this the bar-spinner and the treble hook masked by the hairwing and the overall length could be over 15 cm (6 in). The long bar-spinner tube can be extremely effective for salmon in all sorts of weather and water conditions.

# 5

# Commercial Spinners

Commercial spinners are not just lumps of metal stamped out by a machine despite thinking to this effect. There are a great many people in the business of producing quality spinning lures for the discerning fisherman.

### G.M. Lane & Co. (Ireland): Lane Minnow

One of the companies who produce quality spinners and take a pride in their product is G.M. Lane & Co. of Abbeyfeale, Ireland. The 'Lane Minnow' was born when George Lane returned to his native Ireland after working and living in the United States for twenty years. Settling at Abbeyfeale, Co. Limerick and having the river Feale flowing near his home, he was soon fishing on the river banks.

George was a skilled machinist and being generally dissatisfied with the lures of the time, he designed and made his own. For years he experimented with various body sizes and used bright alluring colours for the prototypes. During the winter months he produced the various body shapes and painted them in attractive minnow-like colours. When the spring came around and the fishing season opened, he tried out all the artificial lures he had created during the close season on the salmon and trout, with help from his friends. Slowly he improved the design until the time came that the only spinning bait he used was his own creation.

Many of his friends and acquaintances were also using the Lane Minnow exclusively for the entire season and catching salmon and trout in all sorts of water. In one season George Lane, using his own minnow, caught over 250 sea trout. For George, making minnows during the winter was a hobby but as its fame as a fish catcher spread far and wide, he was overwhelmed by requests for his minnow. The hobby was beginning to become a useful earner.

To meet this demand he started to manufacture the minnow seriously in 1949. There was no doubt the Lane Minnow was building a reputation as something special. It proved to be the perfect lure in many counties and many double figures of brown trout have been taken on it from Lough Erne in County Fermanagh.

It is also an excellent spinner for sea trout in normal fishing conditions and in low water conditions the smaller sizes are very effective, particularly when fished in the fast runs. The most productive method with the Lane Minnow for sea trout in low water conditions, is to throw the minnow upstream and retrieve very quickly. The best place for this method is where the water flow is very quick; the necks and tails of pools and narrow runs. The Lane Minnow is available in four sizes and the following colours: brown/silver, brown/gold, blue/silver, blue/gold, green/silver, green/gold and all gold.

Many years of testing, planning and research went into producing the original Lane Minnow and the design has not changed as it has stood the test of time. One of the outstanding features is its special mount which allows the fish plenty of play without levering against the plastic body. One of the reasons why the Lane Minnow gives excellent results is the great care taken by the manufacturer to ensure that the minnow is perfectly balanced which leads to a good horizontal spinning action. The level swimming action makes it an excellent trolling lure in the loughs and lakes of the world. It is effective in all its sizes for salmon (all species), trout (all species), pike, chub and zander.

As with all successful designs, there are always copies which may be inferior. Before parting with your money check that the product is what it claims to be.

George Lane died in 1973, and the company is now run by his son John who maintains the same high standards. Each lure is inspected by John Lane personally for quality and balance before being dispatched to clients.

## Abu Garcia Limited (United Kingdom)

Abu Garcia ranks as one of the larger tackle makers with outlets in most countries. Although they have a major interest in tackle generally, they do produce a comprehensive range of spinning baits. Some of the lure names are well known to the experienced fishermen.

### Bar-spinners

**Droppen**  The Droppen is one of the leading bar-spinner designs. With the pear-shaped body weight on the stainless steel shank it is very easy to cast. Its action makes it most attractive to all types of predators; it is good for salmon and trout. It is available in five sizes and the following colours: gold, silver, copper, zebra and fluorescent orange. It is also available with coloured flexo tape stuck on the spin blade to improve its visibility in dirty or murky water, reflecting what little light there is.

**Sonette**  Available in three sizes and three colours (silver, copper and zebra), this is a bar-spinner with a sonic call. The special flanges in the spinning blade will emit vibrations which will alert the predator – ideal for pike. On the treble hook a cock hackle dyed hot orange is wound for added attraction.

**Reflex Red and Reflex White**  The bodies are torpedo-shaped and are painted red or white and are available in three sizes and the following colours: silver, copper and zebra. Reflex Red is also available with a gold blade and Reflex White with a fluorescent orange blade. All the Reflex series have dyed hot orange cock hackles wound on the treble hooks for added attraction.

Reflex is an attractive fast spinning lure which is very good in dark waters, but it is best to add an anti-kink vane on your fishing line. The fast rotation of this spinner after a period of use may pose a few problems – especially if the line swivel is not first class. When using this spinner in fast flowing streams the anti-kink vane is a must.

**Morrum Spinner**  Colours: silver, copper, zebra, blue gill and fluorescent orange. This spinner has a compact metal body in front of the pear-shaped spinning blade. The metal body allows it to sink head down and the spinning blade will rotate in a fussy manner. There is a special wire attachment in front to help in protecting the line from the sharp teeth of the fish hitting the lure. For extra visibility the Morrum Flexo can be used in murky waters. It is ideal for most predatory species and is available in three sizes with a hot orange hackle wound on the treble hook.

**Jungle** Bar-spinner in two sizes and two colours, silver and copper, with an attractive jungle cock decoration on the spinning blade. Excellent for trout and salmon.

**Toby Spin** Two sizes in gold, silver, copper and zebra. Lightweight bar-spinner with the easily recognizable toby-shaped blade. Effective for game fish.

## Spoons
When properly used, spoons are a deadly method of taking fish. The biggest problem is that unless the fish has taken it properly there is a good chance this lightly hooked fish will use the bulk of the metal forming the spoon as a lever to slip the hook. After hooking a fish on a spoon always take it easy until you can see how well the fish is hooked. If whole of the spoon is visible it is more than likely the fish is only lipped hooked on one or two of the triangles, and great care will have to be taken if the fish is to be landed.

**Atom** Nine colours and four sizes.

**Atom Giller** One size only and four colours, gold, silver, copper and zebra. The broad spoon of the Atom and Atom Giller with its corrigations reflect the light, giving a very suggestive signal to the fish-hungry predator, sometimes bringing them from quite a distance away. There is no doubt it is a very effective lure for pike. The weed guard on the Atom Giller does make it easier to fish weedy waters.

**Koster** This comes in three sizes, in silver and copper. Koster is an old favourite with the salmon angler, particularly for big rivers in high water. Easy to cast, quick sinking and irregular in action.

**Glimmy** Colours: silver, copper, blue gill, perch scale. It has an attractive action and the fluorescent spot on the spoon will give the predator an aiming point when making their strike. Available in three sizes.

**Salar** Two colours, silver or copper. A must for salmon fishing, good to cast and fishes in an irregular fashion. Three sizes only.

**Salar Trolling** Colours available: silver blue, silver lime green and silver red. A new lure in one size only. Suitable for all trolling in deep or shallow water. Its rapid and irregular swimming pattern is particularly attractive to salmon.

**Toby** In seven sizes, this original design is a very popular lure with most salmon fishermen. I have many memories of fishing with the Toby and the number of salmon I have taken on it is well into double figures. Admittedly I have lost a lot of fish slipping the hooks on this lure. To reduce my losses, I now fish all my spoons with a special trace or tandem treble hook mount; this has up to a point put a few extra fish into the net. It is I think the same old story, if the fish has not taken firmly it is very difficult to avoid them giving a couple of leaps and shedding the hooks. However, this risk has to be taken as spoons are too effective not to be used. You must just hope all your fish have taken it well back into the mouth. Available in many colours.

**Toby Tiger**   Brightly coloured lure in four sizes and two colours, fluorescent yellow and fluorescent orange. Its dark tiger stripes makes it very attractive for salmon and trout, particularly sea trout. In my experiences the orange tiger has the edge but you may find differently; both designs are very effective.

**Toby Fat**   Two sizes and three colours, silver, copper and fluorescent orange. Most effective when retrieved at slow speeds. Its elliptical shape and the double curve of its spoon give it an undulating movement which is very lifelike. This unique and distinct swimming pattern is certainly very effective in attracting the attentions of predatory fish.

**Toby Salmo**   Colours: silver, blue gill, silver lime green, silver red and silver blue. In one size only, this big fat Toby is the high water and big river lure and is also very useful as a trolling lure. Takes most species of large predatory fish including salt water species.

**Toby Trolling**   One size and three colours, silver lime green, silver red and silver blue. This is a new slimline design but still retains the old Toby outline shape. The slimline design has successfully made it more attractive for stillwater trolling. It is an allround lure in the large lakes and is proving to be more than good for salmon and trout as it is for the many other predatory species that inhabit these large expanses of fresh water.

## Delta Tackle (United Kingdom)
Delta produce mainly fishing tackle for the saltwater angler. They also produce a very useful spinning spoon which can be used for both fresh and salt water species.

**Flasha**   In four sizes, this is a chrome spoon with a reflective strip of bright tinsel on the outside of the spoon, which when fishing, twists and turns in the water reflecting the light, giving the effect of a sparkle being emitted from the lure. It is available with many coloured reflective strips; popular colours are green, yellow, blue, orange and red. This is the only design Delta have at the moment but there are several prototypes being tested. No doubt there will be more types available in the future.

## Ragot SA (France)
In 1930 Andre Ragot, a professional fly-tyer, founded the Ragot company and it has grown rapidly. Today Ragot, under the direction of Hubert Guillois, has outlets in many countries and provide a wide range of fishing tackle, including spinners and flies for both fresh- and salt-water fishing, to the anglers of Europe.

**Nessie**   This is available in six colours and two weights; it is made of latex cut to a fish shape with a longshank single hook threaded through the latex to give it an undulating shape. This is attached to a fish-shaped painted metal head which has a treble hook and eye ring where it is joined to the fishing line. This lure is attractive for all predatory species with its undulating action in the water.

**Teaser Nessie**   Same as Nessie apart from fine white fins at the sides just behind the head.

**Maurice Laurens Brochet**   Its construction consists of two stainless steel wire shanks; the first shank has a fish-shaped metal head threaded on it which provides the casting weight. On the second shank is a red plastic body and spinning blade, which spins directly on the shank. The treble hook is dressed with a red wool tail. Its silver spinning blade has a fish-scale type finish with a red or orange reflective spot on the bottom end. It is available in four sizes. Because of its design the blade will spin slowly as it sinks after a cast. Good for pike and zander, it will also take most other predatory fish.

**Spirala**   It is constructed from a stainless steel wire shank on which is slid a fish-shaped length of thin latex-type plastic with a spiral twist and fine short feelers on the edges to impart life. The head is a fish-shaped piece of metal with eye ring and treble hook. At the business end is an orange or red bead and a latex-dressed treble hook. The action of this spinner is unique, giving the impression of continuous movement as it spins on its stainless steel wire shank. It comes in two weights and six colours, with the head painted red or yellow with black eye. Useful for all predators, fresh or salt water.

**Yann Spoon**   Heavy nickel spoon designed for a wide range of applications in both fresh and salt water. Available in fourteen sizes. The smaller sizes are suitable for freshwater species. Very useful for heavy water fishing for salmon.

**Mirroyann**   Simular to the Yann except one side is covered with a multi-coloured reflective material which gives a sparkle effect to the whole spoon. Good for deep and coloured waters. Available in eight sizes. Excellent salmon and pike lure.

## John L. Hildebrandt Corporation (USA)

In 1899 John L. Hildebrandt, known locally as 'Big John', started the company which is now known as the Hildebrandt Corporation in Logansport, USA. By trade John Hildebrandt was a plumber but he was also an avid fisherman and experimented with different ways of catching fish. One of the results of his experimental work became what is now known as the original Hildebrandt spinner. He made the original from a one dime coin suitably given a curved shape, and one of his wife's hairpins for the shank. This simple design proved to be very effective in taking fish in his local waters. His fame as a top fisherman gradually spread as also did his spinners. This created such a demand for his lures from the local fishermen that he had to give up plumbing and start earning his living tackle-making. He knew from his experience as a plumber that only quality materials and workmanship would ensure success. This policy was implemented from the beginning with creative innovation combined with quality and made Hildebrandts the pioneers of many designs which are now considered to be the normal standard in the tackle industry today. Big John passed this philosophy on to his son Hiram who took over running the company. Hiram directed the company for forty-two years during which time it grew and maintained its tradition of excellence.

In 1925 a spinner called the 'Slim Eli' was developed. This spinner became the flagship of the company, showing the quality of their products. Most of the manufacturing of the spinners is done by hand. The bar-spinner is constructed with a rustproof stainless steel wire shank. The top loop is fashioned neat and tight, with no cut end protruding to catch the fishing line and perhaps cause a loss of a fish. It has a nickel-plated brass clevis which never rusts and always spins freely. There are two brass bearings lowerside of the clevis to ensure the hand polished blade has a smooth spinning action.

Automated manufacturing does not always reduce the cost of production. Hildebrandt in the pursuit of excellence still do the bulk of their manufacturing by hand. This allows quality control in each stage of the product manufacture to be carefully monitored. Any changes in design can be quickly implemented without the cost of adapting a machine which can only produce as programmed.

In due course Hiram's two sons, John and Alan came into the business. John took over directing the company in 1954, still pursuing the policy as laid down by his grandfather. During John 2nd's time, many more designs were developed and his pledge was: 'We absolutely guarantee materials and workmanship to be right. If you ever get a defective lure or spinner from Hildebrandt, return it for a replacement at no charge.'

After John 2nd retired, the running of the company was taken over by Alan's son, Mark, the fourth generation of Hildebrandts to continue the tradition of the past ninety-two years (at the time of writing) of quality and excellence.

**Tornado**  The Tornado's counter spinning blades create a vibration in the lure which sends a call to the fish in the area. Its design consists of a stainless steel shank on which the first bodyweight is placed, then the bearing and spinning blade, followed by another bearing and bodyweight, then the second spinning blade which is designed to spin in the opposite direction from the first. The treble hook is added via a split ring. A fly pattern can be dressed on this hook: fly pattern tails do improve its fish-taking qualities. It is effective for most species of fresh-water fish and can be trolled or spin cast on lake or river. Available in one size, gold or silver.

**Rabbit Foot**  A bar-spinner available in three sizes with a gold or nickel spinning blade and body of gold or nickel with a treble hook dressed with fly pattern or bare. An outstanding spinner, it is a great favourite with fishermen for taking trout and pan-fish.

**Spin Star**  A front weighted spinner with a soft plastic tail, single hook or fly treble hook. Available in one size in gold or nickel. Fly hook colours: yellow, white, black and yellow. Soft plastic tail colours: chartreuse, white, red and white, black and red.

This is a bar-spinner design with the difference of having the weight in front of spinning blade. Its action starts as soon as it hits the water. It is a good lure for trout, crappie and pan-fish, and makes an excellent lure for the beginner learning the rudiments of the art of spinning.

**Switcheroo**  This bar-spinner has a bottom snap loop which allows the fisherman to 'switch' tails, flies or hooks in seconds. It is a weighted spinner in two sizes, gold or nickel.

Having the flexibility to change the hook easily and quickly gives the angler the ability to cover the complete range of fish species: he can adjust or change the lure to suit whatever conditions are prevailing.

**Front Runner**   A small front weighted bar-spinner with single hook tail. One size only, in gold or nickel with two tail styles, Grub Bug and Wee Worm. Colours: Grub Bug, yellow, white or chartreuse; Wee Worm, yellow, white, black, purple or chartreuse.

A useful little spinner with a fussy action, suitable for trout and pan-fish. There is fast rotation of the spinning blade when it is retrieved at slow speeds.

**Wicked Widow**   A bar-spinner which features a twin wire weed guard close to the hook, thus allowing it to be used in a lightly weeded environment. With care when retrieving, it is surprising how well it can be fished into the weedy cover. Available in two sizes, gold or nickel with a vinyl skirt and a wide choice of colours.

**Whizzo**   Weighted lure with its body in front of the June Bug blade. Good for trolling, drifting or cast fishing. The June Bug blade will spin at the slowest of retrieves. Useful for pike, walleye and trout.

Available one size only in the following body colours: nickel, gold, pearl white, green, fluorescent red/white, chartreuse and green/chartreuse.

**Wallbanger**   An effective drift lure with its body weight in front of June Bug blade. Ideal for any fish, it can be fished or retrieved at any depth. It is a particularly effective lure when fished on the drift from a boat. Designed for the walleye but takes other species equally as well. It comes in two sizes with numerous body colours.

**Snagless Sally**   As the name suggests, this is a bar-spinner with weed guards for its keel-weighted custom hook with its vinyl skirt. Available in four sizes with gold or nickel spin blades.

This lure has been around for over fifty years and is a great favourite with bass fishermen in the United States, and I suspect elsewhere. The original Sally, or rather Yellow Sally, had a long dyed yellow fibre hackle wrapped around the hookshank in a attempt to make it weedless. There is no doubt that this lure has stood the test of time and it is one of those rare lures that can be fished in any way to suit the water: deep or shallow, fast or slow, it will make no difference.

For deep fishing, just cast the lure out between the weed banks and allow it to settle on the bottom in open water. When ready, after the disturbance of the cast has settled down, lift it off the bottom and retrieve it just fast enough to make the spinner work. The occasional twitch or jerk can be a useful tactic.

To fish the Sally as a surface lure, cast it out and retrieve immediately, running or bulging the lure just under the surface. This is a useful tactic for rainbow trout and also works well in heavy weed beds. Fish the lure over them fast until there is a spot of clear water, then let it sink deeper in case a fish has been following.

Alan Hildebrandt explained that about twenty-five years ago they added the wire weedguards to the original design to improve its effectiveness in weed. Therefore Yellow Sally refers to the lure without wire weed guards and Snagless Sally refers to the lure with the wire weedguards.

Currently Hildebrandt produce over two hundred types of spinners for a wide range of freshwater fishing, many of them specialist lures for particularly tough conditions, time of year or species of fish. Hildebrandt takes the view, with which I totally agree, that of all the artificial lures, the spinner/fly combination has probably been the most consistent fish-taker over the entire fishing season year in and year out.

## Rapala (Finland)

Vibrax spinners, produced at the Rapala Heinola factory in Finland, are a basic bar-spinner design with the addition of the church bell effect. The construction is a stainless steel shank with treble hook at one end; the Vibrax gear which counter-rotates is now placed on the shaft, followed by the bell-shaped cover. Next are the brass bearings, clevis and spin blade. The spinner is now finished off with its eye loop.

When the spinner is being fished the Vibrax gear inside the bell rotates and strikes – thus emitting high-frequency sonic calls – which will alert any predators that are in range.

**Vibrax Original**   Available in seven sizes and four colours, silver, gold, copper and black. The all-black version is very effective in clear water for trout.

**Vibrax Fluorescent**   Six sizes and five colours, SFY, SFR, CFR, GFR and BFR. The fluorescent yellow and red bell bodies make good aiming points for attracting fish. Certainly the BFR version is quite deadly with its fluorescent red bell-shaped body and black coloured spin blade for game fish.

**Vibrax Foxtail**   Gold or silver with attractive hair tails dressed on the treble hooks, in five sizes. Colours are:
SXR:   silver with red hair tail
SXY:   silver with yellow hair tail
GXR:   gold with red hair tail
GXY:   gold with yellow hair tail

A good bar-spinner and fly tail combination, very effective for salmon, trout, steelhead and sea trout, particularly when fresh-run. This combination with the sonic call wakes up the rainbow trout as well as many other predators.

**Vibrax Decorated**   A bar-spinner in two colours, gold or silver. The spinning blades are decorated with red spots which gives added attraction to the lure as it is being fished. Good for all game fish. Available in five sizes.

**Vibrax Whisper**   Available in gold or silver, in four sizes. The specially designed spinning blade gives out vibrations when being fished. Excellent for all species.

**Inkoo Spoons**   These come in five weights and nine colours. Immaculate paint finish with well designed shape. Excellent for all species.

## Lindquist Bros Bait Co. Ltd (Canada)

In addition to the Canadian Wigglers, Lindquist Bros also produce a fish-shaped spoon lure, named Cisco, which is available in four sizes: 13 cm, 8 cm, 4 cm and 3 cm, and the same colour range as the Wiggler.

The Cisco is a lure that performs well in all sorts of conditions. It can be fished with rod and line, or trolled. It is claimed that it is possible to troll the Cisco up to eight miles an hour without destroying its action. Just open up the motor and watch the results – at these speeds the Cisco will maintain its fishing pattern, flicking, rolling and darting from side to side.

When using it with rod and line it can be fished in fast currents or still waters. When retrieving fast or slow, it will maintain its fishing pattern. The more it is played with, the more attractive it is to fish.

For best results on rod and line, let the lure sink after casting it out. It will sink erratically, flicking as it does. Combine this with the sink and draw technique, varying the retrieve with slow or fast pulls on the draw. Good for all predators, the Cisco is designed as an imitation of the herring or minnow.

## Dexter Lures (Wales)

Dexter was founded in 1932 and in 1972 it extended into the manufacture of fishing tackle. A comprehensive range of spinning lures is now produced for fresh- and saltwater fishing.

**Menai Spoon**  Available in three lengths, all colours – heavy or lightweight: 65 mm/13 g, 65 mm/8 g, 78 mm/13 g, 78 mm/20 g, 90 mm/29 g, 90 mm/18 g. A useful salmon lure.

**Long Spoon**  Five sizes: 27 g, 32 g, 40 g, 60 g and 85 g. An excellent salmon spoon – particularly for high water fishing in rivers. It is useful for fishing the fast water at the tail of a pool. To slow the action of this spoon, reverse the swivel so that the broad end of the spoon is leading. Pike will often go for this slow fluttering movement. Colour can be sometimes an important factor for pike. Available in the full range of colours.

**Ogwen**  Smaller brother of the long spoon. Available in three sizes: 39 mm/7 g, 50 mm/11 g and 65 mm/16 g.

**Conway Spoon**  Traditional spoon and a great favourite of mine, particularly the gold/black zebra with one of my yellow hackle treble hook fly tails on its business end. Excellent spoon for the slower pools, when fished in the correct manner. Three sizes: 40 mm/7 g, 50 mm/11 g and 65 mm/16 g. Available in all colours and throughout its range it is effective for all predators.

**Spindex**  Bar-spinner – available in all colours and six sizes. The spin blade will revolve freely even at slow retrieve speeds.

**Dexter Devon Minnow**  These Devons vary from the traditional minnow, inasmuch as they are considerably heavier for their size. This is due to the fact they are turned out from a solid brass bar. Larger sizes have their mounts fitted with a Dexter double swivel which gives them an excellent rotation action. Four sizes: 38 mm, 52 mm, 64 mm and 77 mm. Available in all colours.

**Dexter Wedge**  An unique lure, extremely effective because of its shape and fish-appealing wobbling swimming pattern in all types of waters. Takes all species equally well from fresh or salt waters. Available in six sizes and all colours.

The first time I fished the Wedge was four or five years ago. I was using a silver

Wedge with one of my blue Flashabou treble hook fly tails for sea trout. The results on that day and since have been good. I have tried it with various fly tails for game fish and I have been most impressed by its effectiveness and its unique fishing movement. I hear some anglers have been connecting two or more wedges together and are getting excellent results, particularly when sea fishing. It may be a good idea to leave the treble hook on the middle split ring; it will certainly improve the hooking capacity of the tandem lure.

**Mackerel Spinner**   Designed for saltwater fishing, these spinners are also useful for freshwater trolling, particularly if fitted with tandem treble hook fly tails. Dexter Mackerel Spinners are mounted on a stainless steel wire centre bar which ensures effortless free spinning action. A relatively cheap spinner – good for using in situations where because of the hazards tackle losses are high. When fitted with fly tails, they are excellent for all freshwater predators – probably all saltwater species as well.

**Dexter Lure Colours**   Gold, copper, silver, zebra, blue, yellow, green, red, purple, orange and black. Most of the lures are a combination of colours and patterns. The colours I have given are the main colour of the lure.

6

# More Spinners

**Bruce & Walker Ltd (United Kingdom)**
It was in 1964 that Jim Bruce, rod maker, moved from London to the village of Upwood, Cambridgeshire, where he joined with Ken Walker to form the company of Bruce & Walker Ltd, developing and supplying fishing tackle, including the following spinners to anglers.

**Norway Dimple Spoons** Three sizes: Lightweight, 20 g; Mediumweight, 24 g; Heavyweight, 35 g.

**Harkin Dublin Spoons** Four sizes: Harkin Boy Lightweight, 10 g; Harkin Boy Mediumweight, 12 g; Harkin Man Lightweight, 14 g; Harkin Man Mediumweight, 19 g.
   Colours: silver, gold, blue/silver, copper/silver and red/gold.
   These are useful spoons for salmon and all species of trout in most conditions, and very effective pike lures when used in the right situation.

**Devon Minnow Round** Available in seven sizes and eleven colours, green/yellow, blue/yellow, blue/silver, blue/green, black/silver, green/gold, brown/yellow, orange/brown, red/gold, brown/gold and black/gold. Available with or without copper tube or mounts.

**Devon Minnow Flat** Four sizes, colours as above.

Devon minnows have truly stood the test of time. Who the originators were or when it was devised I do not know. There are references to the Devon minnow in fishing literature well back into the last century. The early Devons were fearsome lures with mounts just bristling with hooks. Devon minnows of today just have the single treble hook on the mount; occasionally you may see one with a tandem treble hook mount.
   Early season salmon anglers tend to favour the Devon minnow in the cold waters of the early spring. Fish at this time of year like to lie deep, and will only move slowly if tempted by a large lure that has been presented correctly to them, hence the need to fish slowly and deep. Unfortunately early spinning for salmon by many anglers is largely ineffective because of their lack of basic knowledge. Spinning for early season salmon in cold water is highly skilled; it is not a skill learned overnight, it takes practice and experience.
   The angler of today probably has a wider selection of Devons and plugs at his disposal that fish well in cold early conditions than ever before. However the correct choice must be made if you are to be successful. To illustrate this, just imagine the action of a lightweight Devon in a strong flow of water in early spring. In this type of water the Devon will be fishing too high in the water, the movement

will be good but it will be travelling too fast and over the top of fish, which as a rule in cold conditions will not move fast for it. To make it fish correctly it will be necessary to add weight. There are two ways this can be achieved: either add weight on the line or change to a heavier spinner. Be careful about choosing the heavier spinner as if the minnow is not correctly balanced it will not swim on an even keel. The disadvantage of using heavy Devons, even properly balanced ones, is that it is not possible to adjust its weight for the different depths and currents in a pool. The swimming pattern of a heavy Devon is never as good as the light Devon which will work in the current, particularly if there is weight on the line to achieve the depth. An unbalanced minnow will only work correctly in a fast current where the pull of the fishing line and the fast rotation of the minnow will keep it on a level keel. In slow water and at slow retrieving speed the tail – the business end of the minnow, will drop. This will put the angler at a disadvantage should a fish hit the lure as the treble hook is not where it should be, and means that the fish bumping the spinner could be pricked instead of being hooked. Fishing near the river bed with the minnow in the tail down position increases the risk of being snagged up.

Unbalanced Devon minnows are only able to swim on an even keel in fast water or at fast retrieve speeds, which handicaps the angler on every cast. The easy way of overcoming this is to place a split-shot of the correct weight on the fishing line in front of the minnow's nose. Another more permanent method of ensuring that a minnow will swim correctly at all times is to wind lead wire on the front of the minnow's hook mount.

My normal method of fishing the Devon minnow is to select a plastic or wooden minnow, the colour depending on conditions. On the fishing line 60 cm (2 ft) away from the minnow I will add a weight suitable for the depth and current of the water I am fishing. I cast the minnow across the river, slightly upstream from where I am standing and allow it to come around in the current, occasionally letting the lead bump the bottom, at the same time being careful to avoid it driving into the bottom and snagging. Fishing in this fashion allows the wooden or plastic minnow to flutter about 30 cm (1 ft) or so off the river bed.

The technique of using weight on the fishing line gives good control, enabling you to adjust your minnow to fish whatever depth is required for the speed of the current in front of you. In fast water, add weight, in slow water, take weight off. This will ensure that with every cast the minnow is presented to the fish deep and slow with the correct swimming action. No wasted cast, one hundred per cent fishing action.

Next time you go early spring salmon fishing, observe your fellow anglers; it will not be difficult to see who the skilled fishers are. Spinner or fly, for early salmon the technique must be slow and deep.

## Landa Sports Ltd (United Kingdom)

For twenty years Tony Perrin worked for a major fishing company, manufacturing, developing and marketing a range of products, of which many became known worldwide. Following the takeover which led to reorganisation of the manufacturing base of the company in the late seventies, Tony took the decision to go his own way, thus having the freedom to develop his ideas fully.

In 1983 he founded Landa, of Charnock Richard, Lancashire. Within a year had made a good start as a specialised lure manufacturer. His first lure the 'Lukki', was developed to compete in the market he had originally created. Just eight years after the launch Landa has achieved a significant share of the market within Europe.

**Lukki Spoon**    This is available in seven weights. To improve presentation, the spoon blade has been slimmed down on one edge and the lower fin on the bottom end of the blade has been slightly increased in size. The other fin is positioned mid-way on the blade like a dorsal fin and is smaller. This arrangement leads to sixty per cent of the blade's mass hanging below the lateral line, causing the lure to kick over more regularly and with a more natural side-on presentation, without having to speed up or change the direction of the retrieve to achieve this. The improved fishing action of this design and its more natural presentation has not only made it more attractive to the fish, but has improved its hookability. Another advantage of the slimmed down blade edge is that it cuts through the water easily, having less tendency to rise when swinging across a faster flow of water.

Extremely good for salmon in all waters, from spinning to trolling, the Lukki has eye and scale finish on both sides of the blade, and boasts of fourteen colour options in almost every size.

Tony Perrin confidently remarks: 'Lukki had to be bright and stay bright too, hence the decision to vibro polish the blades prior to electroplating "Gold" and copper finishes by the expensive "vat" process, i.e. individually wired up for plating and unwired afterwards. This compares with others who only bulk polish the blades before painting directly onto the brass or copper substrate with the result that, over a short time, the brass and copper lures "patinate" and go dull – even in store before sale.

'We can confidently guarantee that Lukki lures will never degenerate in this way even after many month's continuous immersion in saltwater. Lukki "silver" finish is also vat chromed (copper + nickel + chrome) rather than just barrel nickeled (a much cheaper bulk process).'

Tony then continues: 'After experimenting with various types of lacquers the latest technology translucent epoxy system was finally chosen even though it required stoving twice at high temperatures. First to "lock" the hand-painted colours and secondly, after auto-lacquer dipping, the final clear coating. The resultant finish is "as tough as old boots" and is extremely difficult to remove except by hard physical scratching with a sharp instrument.'

**Turbo**    The same blade shape as the Lukki but with specially designed flow vents in the blade. As the lure is 'fished' through the water, it draws water through the vents, creating a turbulent wake which gives off vibrations. Water jets being forced through the vents and colliding with each other not only cause a turbulent wake behind the spoon but also causes drag to the lure – which allows the lure to be 'fished' more slowly while still presenting lively attraction to the predators. Available in two weights, it is extremely effective for salmon right through its range of eight colours.

**Herri**    Slimmer version of the Lukki without the fins but rather more dense proportions. Available in six weights, it is good for long casting and is suitable for heavy water in rivers and a useful lure in saltwater. The larger sizes have reflective strips of fish scale for added attraction. Good for salmon, trout and all the predatory saltwater species across its eight colour range.

## Colour code for Lukki, Turbo and Herri spoons

| Code | Colours | Water or Weather |
|------|---------|------------------|
| GO | Gold | Dull weather, coloured water |
| GB | Gold/Black | Dull weather, clear water |
| GG | Gold/Green | Dull weather, misty water |
| GK | Gold/Kopper | Clear weather and water |
| GS | Gold/Silver | Coloured water |
| GT | Gold/Tiger | Any conditions |
| FT | Fluorescent/Tiger | Dark or dirty water |
| BF | Black/Flash | Clear conditions |
| KO | Kopper | Clear conditions |
| KB | Kopper/Brown | Clear/low water lure |
| KF | Kopper/Flash | Slightly coloured water |
| ZB | Zebra | Bright weather, clear water |
| SB | Silver/Blue | Dirty water lure |
| SL | Silver | Bright weather, dirty water |
| SF | Silver/Fluorescent/Orange | Dark or coloured water |
| SR | Silver/Red | Dark or murky water |
| SS | Silver/Stripe | Misty to green water |

The colours given for the different conditions are related to river fishing and are only as a general guide. Light and water conditions will alter minute by minute and it is impossible to lay down a guaranteed formula.

**Pikko Spoons**
A traditional broad-bladed spoon that is normally the first choice for pike and salmon fisherman. A useful tactic I have often employed after fishing down the pool for salmon first time with no success, is to change to a broad spoon, particularly one with a red tail or small bangle blade on the split ring; this will sometimes provoke a salmon to strike. Bangle blades can be cut from any suitable plastic bottle and added on any spoon.

**Fatta**
Available in four weights and blade sizes. A compact and punchy allrounder that is attractive to all predators. Useful in lakes and slow flowing rivers, it can be retrieved quite slowly at any depth. It is extremely good for the early season when fished slow and deep for salmon who at that time of year are not prepared to chase or move very quickly. Four colours with small red bangle blades on split ring.

**Thina**
Larger slimmer blade that casts well and can be fished at any depth and speed. Great trolling lure for the predators of the lakes – can be fished very slowly. Available in five colours, one weight only.

**Longa**
The daddy of the Pikko family, the lure to choose for big fish and deep or fast flowing water. It comes in two weights and is available in five colours. Pikko spoons have a superb natural finish showing the prey fish colours to perfection. Extremely effective for salmon (all species), trout (all species), pike, zander and perch.

**Colour code for Pikko spoons, Fatta, Thina, and Longa**

| | |
|---|---|
| GR | Golden Rudd |
| BT | Brown Trout |
| PK | Pikelet |
| YP | Yellow Perch |
| SD | Silver Dace |

**FlipZ**   The FlipZ is a bar-spinner with a water-drop-shaped spinning blade, that runs on a small clevis to ensure minimal friction and fast rotation for the maximum vibrations. Available in the following colours with bangle blades on the business end. Colour code, GS, SF, GK, GB and GO.

It is a very good looking spinner, more than suitable for all predatory species. All the spinning blades have a very attractive eye design on them which will flash signals to the hunters. The SF version would be extremely effective for trout in green or misty water, especially sea trout.

Finally Tony Perrin has joined the FlipZ to Lukki or Herri spoons in tandem creating a bar-spinner and spoon combination that gives the fussy action of the bar-spinning blade in front, followed by the fish-appealing side to side and kick over action of the spoon lure. This makes irresistible lure for all predatory fish because of its alluring movement and its physical length. Long lures and spinners are always attractive to salmon, pike and large trout.

**Lukki + FlipZ Tandem**   Three weights and four colours, GG, KB, SF, SB.

**Herri + FlipZ Tandem**   Three weights and four colours, GO, KO, SF and SB. This combination is also good for saltwater species and sea trout in estuaries and sea lochs.

## Shakespeare Company (UK) Ltd
In 1963 the holdings of Allcock's and Young were taken over by Cope Allman to form Top Tackle. This in turn was acquired in 1965 by the Shakespeare Corporation and formed the foundation for the development of their UK operation. In the following years Shakespeare's growth in the UK was rapid, making it necessary for them to move their operations several times, each time into larger premises to cope with the new developments and increased manufacturing capacity. Shakespeare became brand leader in the UK in 1981, and worldwide have outlets in virtually every country where sport fishing is practised.

### Shakespeare Spinners
The following spinners are all of the bar-spinner design, with different shaped blades and bodies.

**Jet**   This spinner is particularly effective for trout and perch. Finished with a reflective scale effect blade, it is firmly established as one of the Shakespeare's all-time great lures, a very tempting mouthful for all predators. It comes in five sizes, 2, 4, 6, 8, and 10 g, with a wide variety of spinner blade colours.

**Pearl**   A good low-water spinner for salmon and sea trout; also rainbow trout like them, particularly if you add a treble hook with a fly dressed on it. There are five sizes: 2, 4, 6, 8, and 10 g, and the colours are gold/green, silver/red, silver and gold.

**Marble**   Very useful spinner for dull days and still water for perch and jack pike. The spin blades are crimped – in gold or silver – with bright red feathered dressed treble hooks. This spinner would be a particularly useful addition for the sea trout fisher's armoury. Available in four sizes.

**Dorado**   This bright spin blade in silver/black/red or silver/black/yellow is good for all types of spinning. Four sizes: 2, 3, 5, and 7 g.

**Ilbe Spinners**   Shakespeare have introduced this superb range, available in many colours, which have proved to be so successful in Europe for freshwater and saltwater predators. They have a willow-shaped spin blade.

**Kilko**   A bar-spinner with a pear-shaped spin blade, colours zebra, gold/red, silver/red, silver/blue. This superb pike lure, aerodynamically styled for distance casting, has been very successfully taking its full share of bass, pike and game fish. Three sizes: 5, 10 and 15 g.

## Mepps SA (France)

Mepps spinners have been produced since 1938 and are famous world wide. I became aware of the Mepp spinner in the early fifties where they proved to be extremely effective for taking game fish in my local rivers.

Colour and decorations are very important in lure design and all the classical Mepps spinners have their spinning blades in two basic colours, gold and silver plus two complementary colours, black and copper.

All the motifs on the blades are not merely decorative but give visual allure to the fish. Experience has shown that the basic metal blade with a decorative design of black or blue dots, red spots or bands and fluorescent colours, will allow the fisherman to tackle a wide range of water and weather conditions and will take 'fish' if his choice has been correct.

There are always anglers who will fish one favourite type of lure regardless of conditions. When this happens the lure will only work well when used in conditions that suits its characteristics. For the angler who studies the water and light conditions and adjusts his choice of lure accordingly, the chances of taking fish is very much improved.

The general recommendation for choice of blade colours for various conditions is that silver or gold would be most suitable for poor light conditions and cloudy or muddy water; copper and black are more suited for clear water and good light conditions, as under brilliant sunshine these colours do soften the blade flashes which in gold or silver might put the fish off. A useful tactic in clear conditions is to try copper after gold, and in bright sunlight, black after copper. In low clear water conditions the black blade spinner in the small sizes can be quite deadly for trout.

An important factor in spinner design is the blade shape, which will determine the action of the spinner. Mepps bar-spinners have a different angle of blade rotation for each model, ranging from 25 degrees right through to 60 degrees. Each model, depending on its blade shape and angle of rotation produces its own vibratory effect which can be felt by the angler as he fishes the spinner around on the retrieve in the current. The intensity of the vibratory waves emitted from the various Mepps models differ from each other. It is this frequency vibration that defines the signature of each model of spinner.

Mepps spinners are sized from 00, 0, 1, 2, 3, 4, 5, 6, 7, with 00 being the smallest size.

**Aglia** The Aglia was the first model produced by Mepps and the first bar-spinner that I used. It is available in seven sizes and four colours, gold, silver, copper and black. Optional extras are a treble hook with red pompon or a single hook with red pompon.

**Aglia Decoree** Available in sizes 1, 2, 3, in silver blade with red or blue spots, gold blade with red or black spots, copper blade with red or black spots. Aglia and Aglia Decoree are very effective for most species of fish, particularly trout.

**Aglia Fluorescent** There are six sizes and four colours, rose, chartreuse, orange and white. The peculiarity of a fluorescent blade is that it becomes visible when subjected to ultraviolet rays which have penetrated the deeper water. Because of the depth all other visual signals are extinguished but the fluorescent blades are still actively reflecting the ultraviolet rays, thus inviting attack from the killers of the deep. They are also particularly good in poor light conditions and cloudy water.

The angle of the blade rotation of the Aglia blade from its axis to maximum is 60 degrees. This gives a medium wake effect rather like the wake of a small boat moving very slowly. This rotation creates an intense and vibratory effect to the spinner with maximum drag.

**Anglia TW** Available in five sizes 0, 1, 2, 3, 4, with blade colours of silver/red with black spots, gold/red with black spots or copper/red with black spots. This model is designed so that the treble hook can be changed or the tandem treble hook minnow mount can be added. This minnow mount is available in assorted sizes and colours. Those readers who are fly-tyers can dress their own single and tandem hooks for this spinner. Full details on how to do this is given in Chapter Four.

This spinner is good for all species when used with just the bare treble hook. However when the minnow tandem mount is added it has proved irresistible for all the major predators. After a few fish have been taken the minnow imitation on the treble hooks usually look the worse for wear.

**Winner** Five sizes: 1, 2, 3, 4, 5. Colours are silver/red or gold/red with black bars. Its design makes it possible to change the hooks. The standard model is available with normal treble or single hook with pompon.

**Elix** Colours: silver or gold; five sizes: 1, 2, 3, 4 or 5.

**Elix Fluorescent** Five sizes: 1, 2, 3, 4 or 5. Colours: black/chartreuse, copper/orange, silver/chartreuse, gold/orange.

**Elix Fluorescent Mouche** Same sizes and colours as above. The treble hooks are dressed with orange hackles for the copper and gold spin blades; light blue dun for the black and silver spin blades.

The Elix spinner blade is mounted directly on the shaft without a clevis thus allowing the blade to spin very freely, permitting slow recovery of the lure. The reverse double hollow drop-shape of the blade generates a wide range of sound waves and vibrations, thereby alerting and attracting the attention of even the most wary and suspicious fish. Good for pike and zander, it will take all species if it is used when conditions are suitable.

**Lusox**   Available in four weights, 4, 7, 10 and 13 g, and two blade colours, silver or gold with black stripe and red spot on the end of blade. This spinner is designed especially for pike fishing. The weight for the Lusox is on an independent shaft of stainless steel wire which is attached to the spinner shaft in front of the blade and is removable. One advantage of using a spinner with the weight in front of the blade is that after a cast it will sink head first and the blade will spin while sinking. It always pays to allow the lure a little sinking time before starting the retrieve. Predatory fish are very much attracted to baits that dive or climb; using one 'on the drop' technique after a cast will take fish that will not come to the spinner in the normal way.

To reinforce this point, I recall an incident which happened many years ago. I was spinning for salmon and had fished down the pool once with one spinner. When I was halfway down the pool the second time my reel jammed as a loop of line had somehow caught up behind the bale arm of the reel. Not being able to retrieve the spinner I allowed it to settle on the bottom. It took about five minutes to sort out the line on the reel, then, satisfied all was in order I lifted the spinner off the river bed and started the retrieve. It had travelled no more than a couple of metres when everything went solid; I thought for a moment I had hit a snag in the bottom, then the fish took off and battle was engaged. About ten minutes later I netted a hen fish of 5 kg (11 lb) which had taken the spoon well back in its mouth. This fish had obviously seen the two different types of lure being fished in the normal manner and was not interested. But when I took the spoon off the bottom after it had been lying there for five minutes, the 'on the lift' movement must have provoked it into attacking the lure, which proved to be its downfall.

The Lusox lure, by having the removable weighted stainless steel wire shaft in front of the main spinner shaft, ensures it is more difficult for the fish to slip the hook by levering because it is articulated and the overall length of the two steel shanks keeps the fishing line clear of the fish's teeth. Its triple faced blade with its special shape rotates up to 25 degrees from its axis, produces a medium butterfly action if retrieved at a constant speed.

**Comet Decoree**   Six sizes: 0, 1, 2, 3, 4 or 5. Colours: silver or gold blades with red or blue spots.

**Comet Booster**   Three sizes: 1, 2, or 3. Colours: silver, black, gold or copper.

The Comet series spinning blade has a maximum angle of rotation from its axis of 45 degrees. This is the most active of all the blades, with extra fluttering butterfly actions producing vibrations throughout its retrieve, and generating less drag than the Aglia.

The Comet Booster has the added advantage of the 'ringing bell' body construction which emits its own sonic call in addition to the specific vibrations of the Mepps blade. Its weight is two per cent more than the standard Comet lure in the same sizes. Because of its weight the Comet Booster is very good in rough water and broken currents. This is the heavier Mepps sonic spinner for use in rapid streams that trout and salmon anglers have been waiting for.

**Black Fury**   Available in six sizes with black blades with either red or yellow spots. The blade action is the same as the Comet. It is also available with a fly dressed on a treble hook. It is very good for trout in small streams in clear water conditions; I have found the flytail version deadly for sea trout in clear water conditions during cloudy weather or the last hour before sunset.

*Plate 3*    Big 'S' Plugs, assorted sizes. *Photo: Courtesy Shakespeare (UK) Ltd*

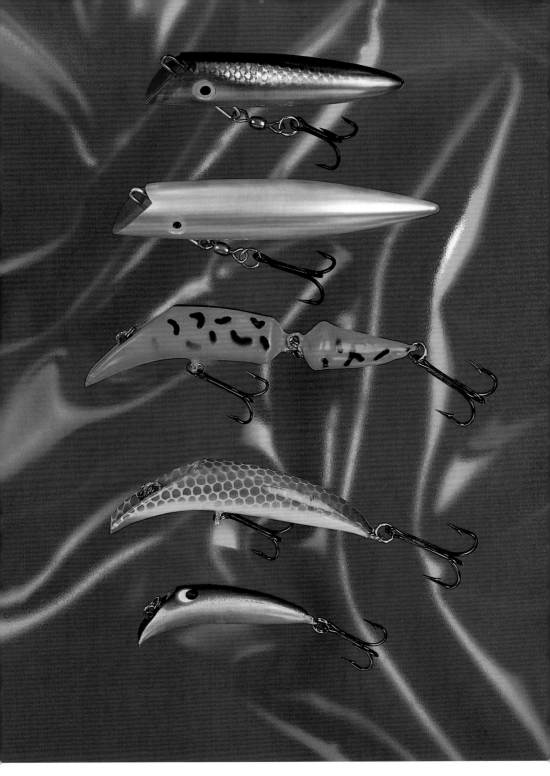

*Plate 4*   Plugs *(from the top)*: Tomic Plug 3 in (7·5 cm); Tomic Plug 4 in (10 cm); Canadian Wiggler – Orange; Canadian Wiggler – Green; Canadian Wiggler – Blue. *Photo: Gordon Bellman*

*Plate 5*  Home-made Spoons and Spinners with fly tails (*from the top*): Copper
Spoon with fly tails; Copper Spoon with fly tails; Green Plastic Spoon; Yellow
Plastic Spoon; Bar-spinner with white plastic tail; Bar-spinner with orange
plastic tail. *Photo: Gordon Bellman*

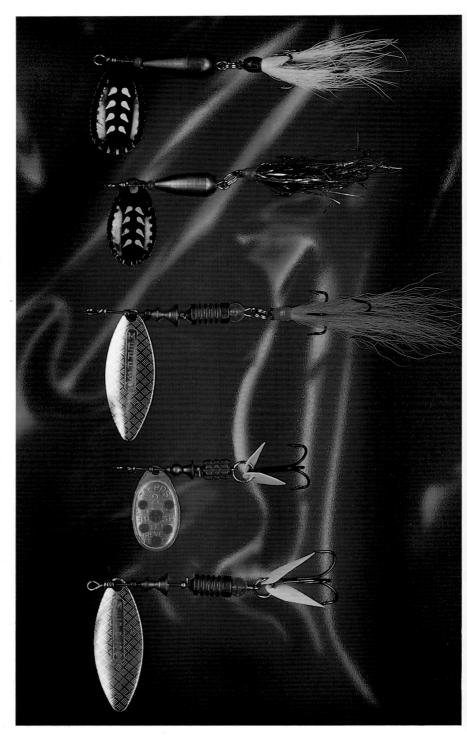

*Plate 6* Bar-Spinners with home-made tails (*from the top*): Black Droppen with white hair tail; Black Droppen with brown and silver Flashabou tail; Gold Mepp with orange hair tail; Gold Mepp with red spots and plastic bangle blades; Gold Mepp with yellow bangle blades. *Photo: Gordon Bellman*

**Comet Rainbo**   Colours: silver, gold or copper, in four sizes: 0, 1, 2, 3. With this model it is possible to change the treble hook easily and a range of options are available for the fisherman: red or white twist tails and an assortment of tandem hook minnow mounts in natural and rouge colours. If the angler makes full use of the various tails and perhaps add a few of his own it would be possible to take predatory fish of virtually any species at any time.

**Aglia Longue**   Four colours, gold, silver, black or copper, available in seven sizes.

**Aglia Redbo**   Colours, gold/red, black/red and silver/red.

**Aglia Rainbo**   Four colours, black, gold, silver or copper.

The blade of the Aglia Long series rotate 30 degrees to its axis due to its willow leaf shape and weight. It has a moderate vibratory effect and good action in all waters and can be fished in relatively heavy water without rising to the surface. It takes all species and is useful for salmon in the larger sizes.

**Giant Killer**   A bar-spinner with a willow-shaped blade in three colours, orange, white or chartreuse. The treble hook is dressed with black tail hair. It is designed for big fish and heavy water, and its weight is 35 g.

**Giant Lusox**   Similar to the smaller version, available in gold/yellow or silver/red with yellow or red hair tails, weight 45 g. Suitable for fishing deep for large lake pike.

**Musky Killer**   Bar-spinner with comet blade in three colours, gold, silver or black, with mixed hair coloured fly tail. Weight 15 g. Good for pike, zander and perch.

**Bass Killer**   This lure is primarily designed for the freshwater bass found in the North American waters. Its design consist of a twin vee-shaped stainless steel wire shank, having on one arm the tandem spinning blades (a small blade followed by a larger one). On the other arm is the hook with its rubber skirt which imparts life to the lure.

The triangular shape of this lure, with its tandem spinning blades on one arm and the attractive vibrations of the rubber skirt on the other makes it a very killing lure for bass. Another advantage of this design is the fact that the single hook swims with the point of the hook upwards thus reducing the chances of snagging, thereby allowing the weedy and difficult stretches of water to be fished properly.

Although designed as a bass lure it has proved to be extremely effective for pike in North America. It is also a good choice for the other predators, zander and perch.

Available in three weights: 9, 10, or 11 g with a choice of spinning blades, Aglia, Willow Leaf and Palette GV (Adjustable Blade), plus a wide variety of rubber skirt colours.

**Mepps 'S' Spoon**   Available in three lengths, gold or silver, in sizes 1, 2 or 3; each size has a lightweight or heavyweight version. The spoon lure bases its efficiency on a totally different concept to the bar-spinner. 'S' spoons depend on good water movement for them to work to maximum efficiency; the 'S'-shaped undulating spoon with a fluted surface has distinct movements in the water. It beats and throbs in all planes and has a side to side sinuous twist in the current.

The larger spoons are a great favourite with the salmon angler; the heavyweight version are very useful in heavy water on big rivers.

**Syclops Spoon**   Seven colours, gold/black, gold/rouge, gold/fluorescent, black/fluorescent, silver/black, silver/rouge and silver fluorescent. These spoons are good for heavy water, shallow runs, fast rapids and heads and tails of pools. They produce the ideal undulating action which, added to their very attractive colours, make them a good choice for game fish. If large fish are expected it may be advisable to change the standard treble hook for a reinforced treble. The Rob Wilson treble code CS9 made by Partridge would be suitable.

**G.V. Bar-Spinner**   This is the same as other bar-spinners apart from the unique spinning blade which can be opened or closed. In the closed position the spinner will run deep, when opened out it will run shallow. This will make it possible to adjust the blade within reason for the water being fished. Available in two sizes and five blade colours, gold, silver, black/silver, gold/silver, black/gold.

**Aglia Flying C**   A bar-spinner with an Aglia-shaped blade with a long weighted stainless steel shank joined to the spinners shank. This shank is covered with a close fitting rubber skirt with two tapering rubber tails which veil the treble hook.

It is available in three weights and four blade colours: gold, silver, black and copper. There are a wide selection of colours for the rubber tube skirts. This design has become very popular for salmon and sea trout spinning and good catches have been reported. It will operate in any type of water at any depth. For really heavy water you will need a powerful rod to fish the 25 g version.

I doubt if Andre Meulnart, when in 1938 he created Mepps with the launch of the Aglia bar-spinner, had any thought that the same design would still be going well and catching fish over fifty years later. The Aglia is now famous world-wide and still represents over forty per cent of Mepps' annual production, which comes out of one plant at Contes near Nice in the south of France. Employing over eighty people under the direction of Jean-Luc Faure, they produce over three hundred spinning patterns which are supplied world wide.

Mepps' development and research departments are constantly designing and testing new products made from all types of materials. These designs are given a long series of laboratory tests before the final testing is done by their experts using the prototypes in real fishing situations.

Any new lures launched by Mepps are the fruits of years of research and testing and have already caught scores of fish before being offered to the fishermen of the world, thus maintaining their position as a leader in design and development.

# 7

# Light Spinners and Fly-Spinners

The design of ultra light or fly-spinners should allow them to be used either with medium to heavy fly rods or lightweight spinning tackle. As the name suggests, the fly-spinner is part fly with the traditional fur and feather dressing and part spinning design made out of metal or perhaps some other material. Some of the fly-spinners are of a sufficient mass to allow them to be used with a light spinning outfit without the need for additional weight on the fishing line. These fly-spinners, if they are used with traditional fly-fishing techniques, would need to be fished on heavy fly lines and powerful fly rods. It is impossible to cast them on flylines and rods that are too light; even with suitable equipment care has to be exercised when making the cast.

## The Fly-Spin Bar Lure

This home-made design is very similar to the normal bar-spinner. The shaft is fine stainless steel, twisted to make a loop at one end. This loop is the business end of the spinner: to this is joined the treble hook on a split ring. Three or four coloured beads are now slid down the shaft. The tube fly is not the normal tube fly with wing and body – this tube fly consists of a narrow piece of plastic tube of 1 cm in length, to which a hair wing is encircled and whipped on, the whole lot being varnished to complete the head. After the tube fly collar, a plastic bead is slid down the shaft which will act as a bearing for the spinning blade. The spinning blade for this design is a little smaller than the blade size normally used for a bar-spinner of this length. Place the spinning blade in the clevis and slide it on to the shaft. Now finish with another bead and twist a loop in the wire to form the eye. Add the treble hook on the business end and the fly-spinner is ready for use. Although the colour combinations are unlimited and the designer can choose any colour that takes his fancy, the following designs are proven and very effective when used correctly in the right conditions.

The overall length of this design including the treble hook, which is veiled by the hairwing, is approximately 8 cm (3 in). If the beads are difficult to acquire use narrow diameter plastic tubing instead.

### Gold and Orange
*Spinning blade*   Gold
*Body*   Orange beads
*Wing*   Tail hair dyed hot orange mixed orange crystal hair

### Gold and Yellow
*Spinning blade*   Gold
*Body*   Clear glass beads
*Wing*   Tail hair dyed bright yellow mixed yellow crystal hair

### Gold and Brown
*Spinning blade*   Gold
*Body*   Green glass beads
*Wing*   Brown tail hair mixed red crystal hair

### Gold and Green
*Spinning blade*   Gold
*Body*   Gold beads
*Wing*   Dyed green tail hair mixed red crystal hair

### Silver and Red
*Spinning blade*   Silver
*Body*   Blue beads
*Wing*   Dyed red tail hair mixed silver crystal hair

### Silver and Black
*Spinning blade*   Silver
*Body*   Clear glass beads
*Wing*   Black tail hair mixed crystal hair

The hook size for the fly-spinner is Partridge X1 size six treble. If so desired, a cock hackle of the appropriate colour can be wound on the treble to give the lure more attraction.

In the early sixties Richard Walker experimented with various materials in an attempt to design a realistic imitation of bait fish in reservoirs. Every year the coarse fish fry, sticklebacks and minnows congregate in the margins of the lakes and reservoirs and large trout who normally do not come in close to the shore make forays into the shallows to mop up the fry thus giving the bank angler a chance to get on terms with them.

Richard Walker, after much experimentation, came up with his polystickle dressing which immediately proved to be a great success. The difference between the polystickle and other fry-imitating lures was the body material. The body of the polystickle was clear polythene, giving the lure a translucency which proved very effective in attracting the trout, especially if the underbody was dressed silver tinsel ribbed red floss. I developed this mode of dressing for my wobblers which are intended to be fished with light spinning tackle or trolled on lakes where this method is permitted.

## Fly-Poly Wobbler
As I needed the Fly-Poly Wobbler to be between 8 to 12 cm (3 to 5 in) long depending on the hook size, I decided the most suitable hook for my requirement was the Carrie Stevens Longshank 10X made by Partridge.

Before dressing the fly-poly, the plastic vane which will determine the lure swimming action has to be whipped into position and secured with glue or varnish. It is very important that the vane is set at the correct angle, that is, looking forward towards the hookeye, also the vane must be straight across the hook-shank. Any slight twist in the vane towards the hookeye or to the sides will induce the fly-poly to spin rather than wobble. This point is not quite so important for the prawn dressing as the plastic tube can be adjusted to the correct action. For the fly-poly, once the lure is completed there is only limited scope for adjustment to the plastic vane.

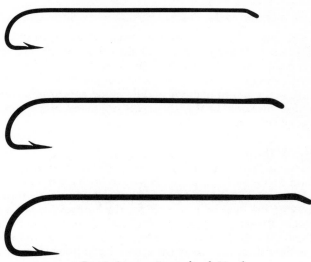

*Carrie Stevens Longshank Hook*

To dress the fly-poly (assuming the plastic vane is already in place close to the hookeye and the glue has fully hardened), cover the hookshank with a bed of silk, then tie in a strip of lead on the underside of the hookshank, pressing the end close up to the vane, which will give it added support. Tie in the raffia tail and back. Wind the underbody of silver tinsel and red floss. Prepare the polythene by cutting it into narrow strips, tie in and wind, pulling the polythene gently as you wind. Shape the body to a nice fish-like shape keeping firm pressure as you wind the polythene, this will give a nice tight body. Do not make the body too fat – when completed tie in the loose end close to the vane. Moisten the raffia back, pulling it tight over the body and secure in front of the vane.

Now tie in a bunch of cock hackle fibres behind the vane to make a false hackle that will veil the belly of the fly-poly. Complete the head, whip finish and varnish. Trim the raffia tail to about 5 cm (2 in) long. The lure is now completed. The technique for dressing the false hackle is to take a bunch of hackle fibres, place into position and tie in as you would a hairwing – except it is under the hookshank not on top as a wing would be.

The overall length of the fly-poly wobbler when dressed on the Carrie Stevens longshank hook makes it an ideal trolling or river spinning lure for which it is best suited. For fishing the margins of lake where this type of lure is allowed, dress the fly-poly on the normal longshank hook which will probably be in keeping with the size of the fry there.

There is no need to change the body of the fly-poly to ring the changes. All that is necessary is to change the colour of the raffia back and false hackle. The following combinations are effective in all sizes from longshank size eight upwards and the Carrie Stevens extra longshank hooks.

**Fly-Poly 1**  *Back and tail*: black raffia. *Hackle*: cock fibres dyed red

**Fly-Poly 2**  *Back and tail*: orange raffia. *Hackle*: cock fibres dyed orange

**Fly-Poly 3**   *Back and tail*: yellow raffia. *Hackle*: cock fibres dyed yellow

A useful tactic when fishing the fly-poly is to cast it out and let it settle on the lake bed. Trout will often pick it up and are caught using this ploy. If after a while nothing has taken the lure, lift it off the bottom and fish it back. The take, if it comes at all, will normally come in the first couple of metres of movement. Poly-stickles both in the spinning mode and fly mode appear to attract the larger fish. The reason for this could be that the larger fish take a bigger portion of their food in the form of small fish and fry.

## Articulated Fly-Wobbler

This lure is constructed in two parts and joined together with a split ring. For the front half, fashion a length of stainless steel wire to form the mount. Take a length of wire about 10 cm (4 in) long and bend it in the middle thus forming a pear-shaped loop, making the loop long enough for the bottom edge of it to protrude out of the lure body. Bend the two ends horizontally from the point where the two wires cross to form the middle loop for the belly treble. At the front where the lure will be tied on to the fishing line, form the eye so that it is vertical. At the rear end where it will be joined to the rear section by a split ring, form the loop eye so that it is horizontal. At the front of the mount, glue in the vane ensuring it is at the correct angle and its face is looking straight ahead. Before forming the rear loop slip on a washer, button or plastic ring about the circumference of a pen. Glue this in place and place the mount to one side and allow to harden.

To prepare the rear section of the articulated wobbler take a size four long-shank straight-eyed hook. Partridge produce an excellent hook called the 'streamer' which is ideal for this purpose. It is very important that the eye of the hook is straight – not up or down. On this hook slip a washer, button or plastic ring about the circumference of a pen tight up to the hookeye and glue into place. After the plastic rings are securely glued in place the next job is to dress the two parts of the wobbler.

Place the front mount in the fly-dressing vice, adjusting the vice jaws so that you are dressing the mount with the vane in the normal looking-down position. Add a strip of weight under the hookshank and whip on, which will ensure the lure fishes correctly in the upright position. Tie in a length of long-fibre chenille and wind tightly to form the body, secure and cut off the surplus, tie in a false hackle behind the vane and whip finish. Varnish the head liberally. To dress the rear portion, re-adjust the vice for the longshank hook. Place the hook in the vice and whip on a bed of silk. Tie in the body material and form the body, remembering to leave enough room for the hairwing. Dress the hairwing encircling the hookshank, making sure the wing is at least twice as long as the hookshank. Complete and varnish in the normal manner. When the varnished heads are hardened off, join the two sections together with the split ring, and add a size eight treble hook to the belly hook holder.

### Articulated Wobbler 1
*Rear hook*   Partridge streamer size 4
*Body*   DFM orange wool ribbed gold oval
*Wing*   Brown bucktail
*Front section*   Brown chenille

*Hackle*   Dyed red cock

**Articulated Wobbler 2**
*Rear hook*   Partridge streamer size 4
*Body*   DFM lime green wool ribbed gold oval
*Wing*   Black bucktail
*Front section*   Black chenille
*Hackle*   Dyed red cock

I have had fish on all sorts of colour combinations using the articulated wobbler. Therefore I am not giving you any more patterns to copy but will leave it to you to devise your own, it is much more fun that way. When making your own mounts do not forget to ensure the rear eye of the front section is horizontal so as to marry to the straight horizontal eye of the streamer hook. Providing the vane has been correctly placed the action of the articulated fly wobbler is unique. The long hair wing moving in the swimming motion is very attractive to predatory fish. It is a very effective lake-trolling lure and good for river fishing.

My next spinning device will allow you to fish any fly-lure as a fly-spinner, and any spinner can be easily used as a tandem spinner. This mount is very simple to make. Take a short piece of stainless steel wire and twist an eye loop at one end and slip on plastic bead. Place the clevis in a spinning blade and slip on a steel wire shank, add another plastic bead and twist the wire to form a loop eye for tying to the fishing line. On the other loop eye you can add a fly lure with a split ring. This device can be used with any fly-lure pattern in circumstances where added flash may be required. It can also be used in front of bar-spinners thus making a tandem bar-spinner or it can be placed in front of a spoon lure for added attraction, thus giving it the necessary weight for use with a spinning outfit. It is very easy to use on fly-fishing tackle when used with only fly lures.

## Fly Spoons
My fly spoon is another lightweight, easy-to-construct design. All that is required is two swivels – one short, the other one long and two split rings. To one end of the short swivel add a split ring, then join on the long swivel. At the other end of the long swivel add the other split ring; this will be the hook ring. Cut the spoon from a stout plastic bottle, using the bottle's shape to impart whatever curve is required. The easiest bottles to cut to shape are the ones made of brightly-coloured flexible plastic which usually hold washing or shampoo liquids. They give the designer the opportunity to create spoons to whatever shape that takes his fancy. At the narrow or top end of the spoon, drill a hole. Join the spoon to the split ring which joins the two swivels and add the treble hook to the split ring on the end of the long swivel.

This spinner can be made with a host of different coloured spoons and dressed treble hooks. Because of its lightweight construction it does not present any problems when being fished with a fly-fishing outfit. The choice of shapes and colours are endless and I will leave it to you to design and test fish whatever you fancy.

I have tested many designs for myself and have been pleasantly surprised how effective they can be. Most useful colours are orange, green, yellow, red, black and white. I have stuck reflective strips of tinsel on to the spoon to add some flash. A white spoon with diamond-shaped reflective tinsel stuck on and a white hackle wound on the treble certainly wakes up the rainbow trout. Before fishing them check you are not breaking any fishery rules. The spoon can be of any size but for the large spoons it will be necessary to construct a mount of stainless steel wire to carry the treble hook.

## Hildebrandt Ultra Lites

The Hildebrandt Corporation manufactures a comprehensive range of fly-spinners and Ultra Lites that can be fished on light spinning tackle or traditional fly-fishing equipment.

**Indiana Spinner**   This is the original spinner designed by Big John over ninety years ago. It is available in nine sizes with single or double spinning blades in gold or nickel. Its construction is a stainless steel shank with a solid brass mirror finish blades on clevises which spin freely on the steel shank. The double blade Indiana spinner has a longer stainless steel shank where the two blades spin in tandem. There is a special clip fastening which will allow a choice of whatever hook is required, from the bare treble to single hooks dressed with flies. These spinners with their various attached hooks are effective right across the freshwater spectrum for all species of predatory fish. In the small sizes they are very good for taking trout in small bushy streams.

**Idaho Spinner**   Similar in construction to the Indiana, the only difference is the blade shape. This blade will spin effectively even at the slowest of retrieve speeds. Nine sizes are available with single or tandem blades. They are finished in bright nickel or gold with the special clip fastening which will allow hooks to be changed quickly and easily, and are effective for all fish.

**Slim Eli Spinner**   This spinner appeared in 1925 when Hiram Hildebrandt was directing the company. It was a remarkable success and became known as the 'Willow Leaf Spinner'. Its construction is the same as the previous spinners and it is available in eleven sizes with single or tandem blades in gold or nickel. The action of its willow-shaped blade is unique; these blades spin close to the shaft creating a vibratory minnow-like action in the water. Used for all types of fishing with hook or fly.

**June Bug Spinner**   The June Bug has a fixed pitch solid brass blade with a riveted blade arm which, when slid on the stainless steel shank, acts like a clevis. Because of the fixed pitch of spin and the blade's shape it can be retrieved at any speed, from dead slow to turbo fast. Available in five sizes, gold or nickel. The hooks can be changed to suit conditions and species of fish.

**Jig Spinner**   Invented in 1960 by John Hildebrandt 2nd, it quickly became a firm favourite with fishermen. It is available in seven Idaho blade sizes, six Willow Leaf sizes, four twin Idaho blade sizes and three tandem Idaho sizes. It has solid brass blades in gold or nickel and is good for all species.

**Little Shaver**   Excellent for fly rod or light spinning, this spoon is available in three sizes and four finishes. The spoon colours can be gold, nickel, chartreuse and fluorescent red. Its construction consists of the brass spoon with a split ring and swivel at the fishing line end. At the other end is a split ring to which a single, treble or dressed hook can be attached – the fisherman's choice. Useful in small streams in wild places for catching breakfast.

**Gondola**   This lure with its long narrow spoon shape has a split ring at the business end to which the treble hook and small flicker blade is attached. Designed primarily for salmon fishing, the minnow-like action of the Gondola is very effective for taking salmon and it also has proved to be deadly for a wide variety of game fish. Large predatory fish such as pike, perch and zander are often taken by it. Available in gold, nickel, pearl, white, chartreuse and fluorescent red. Only one size with 1/0 single hook or treble hook.

**Colorado Spinner**   This spinner is available in six sizes. Construction consists of a swivel front end which is attached to a split ring which in turn is attached to another swivel and spinner blade. On the end of the second swivel another split ring is used to attach the hook. This lightweight, simple to construct spinner, is a great favourite. It is time tested and very effective for taking bass, crappie, pan-fish, brown and rainbow trout. The spinning blades are solid brass, finished in nickel or gold.

**Skinny Dipper**   The Dipper is a useful lightweight bar-spinner for pan-fish and trout, available in one size with gold or nickel blades. The hooks are dressed with three fly patterns – Guinea Red, Squirrel and Guinea Yellow.

**Devil Spinner**   Construction consists of a stainless steel wire body with orange bead and propeller spinning blade in front. The dressed treble hook is secured to the stainless steel wire loop with a split ring. It is available in three sizes and three hackle colours on treble hooks, white, yellow and black. The propeller blade is nickel plated. Good for pan-fish and trout.

**Little Fooler**   Construction is the same as the Colorado spinner except there are two bangle blade flickers on the rear split ring and a vinyl skirt on the treble hook. There is a choice of seventy colours for the skirt which can be mixed to form a multi-coloured skirt. These tail skirts are made of durable vinyl plastic for tough wear and extra long life. The Little Fooler is in two sizes with gold or nickel blades. Effective for pan-fish, brass, crappie and trout.

**Fire Fly**   A very simple design, with construction consisting of a small swivel with a split ring on one end. Attached to this split ring are two bangle blades and a treble hook with a vinyl skirt. When the Fire Fly is moved through the water on the retrieve the bangle blades work like a pair of wings. This movement and the pulsating action of the coloured strands of the vinyl skirt present to the fish a combination which they find irresistible. It is available in one size with nickel bangle blades and a wide choice of skirt colours. Good for lake or river, brass, crappie, pan-fish and trout.

**Shad King**   This is an old design and has been taking fish for well over fifty years. In the past it has been known as the 'Russian Spinner', and sometimes as the 'Shiner'. It is a spoon-shaped lure with a single hook which has two bangle blades on the bend of the hook. Another version is called the Feather Fly which has feathers instead of the bangles. When being retrieved or trolled the Shad King has the lively action of a small bait fish. It comes in eight sizes with gold or nickel blades. For the Feather Fly, the feather colours are white or yellow. Good for all species.

**Flicker Spinners**  The Flicker lure is an old favourite which has been taking bass, crappie, pan-fish, pike and trout for over fifty years. Construction consists of swivel and split ring; the spinner blade and single hook is attached to the split ring, thus forming the lure. Two versions are available, one with bangles on the hook, the other a feather fly design. There are twelve sizes with gold or nickel blades and three fly colours in yellow, white or chartreuse. The bangles on the bend of the single hook certainly impart plenty of movement to the lure. Add to this the movement of the primary spinning blade and it is little wonder that they were given the name 'Flickers'.

Some of the Hildebrandt fly spinners if used with light spinning tackle will require additional weight on the fishing line if casts of any distance are required.

## Mepps SA (France)
The following ultra light spinners are from Mepps of Conte and if properly used they can be a most useful addition for small stream and summer fishing.

**Streamepps**  In one size only, No. 00, with brown, silver or gold Aglia blades. The hook is a wide gape single hook dressed with the following fly pattern:
*Tail*   Red wool
*Body*   Silver tinsel or gold tinsel
*Wing*   Teal
*Head*   Black with white eye dot

The brown and silver blade versions have the silver tinsel body; the gold blade version has the gold tinsel body.
   An easy option for the lure makers who do not have the time to go chasing around looking for suitable stainless steel wire and small spinning blades is to buy the commercially made bar-spinners and hang their own fly designs on the business end of these mounts.
   Small fly-spinners of this type are extremely killing in small streams in clear water and a very useful option for stillwaters where their use is allowed. They can be used with light spinning rod or medium fly rods.

**Aglia Mini Saumon**  Available in one size only, in two colours, fluorescent orange or silver spinning blade. It is of lightweight construction and at the business end is a treble hook which is threaded up through a small plastic minnow and joined to the spinner. It will take pike, perch, rainbow and brown trout and is very effective when the coarse fish fry are swarming in the shallows.

**Mini Rainbo Saumon**  The available colours are silver, gold or copper. It has an Aglia long blade with plastic minnow on treble hook. For use with spinning rod, it is a good running water lure. Fish them in fast rapids and deep holes; it takes those big cannibal trout out of the small streams

## Ragot SA (France)
The Angel lure is produced by Ragot of Loudeac. Its construction consists of a plastic eel glued to a longshank hook and attached to a weighted stainless steel

wire shank on which is a copper spinning blade. It is available in three colours. Useful for trout and salmon, it can also be used for sea fishing.

For the amateur tackle-maker this design can be copied by using Ragot or Delta plastic eels, sticking them on longshank hooks and attaching them to bar-spinners with a split ring. Bar-spinners with this eel tail are very effective for trout in rivers and small streams. Really large plastic eels on a bar-spinner can be useful for salmon, particularly when the elvers are running.

# 8

# Fly-Fishing Tackle

The last forty-five years has seen a steady increase in new waters, created by the building of public water supply reservoirs. These waters in the main have been, over the years, stocked with trout and opened for fly-fishing. With new waters opening up on their doorsteps and increased leisure time, more people have taken up fly-fishing for trout. As their interest in the sport grew, naturally they started to take an interest in fly patterns and how to dress them, and the tackle needed to present them to the fish.

**Fly Lines**
One of the most important areas for the trout fly-fisherman is the choice of fly lines. The various fly lines are designed to perform many roles. The most useful types for the bank angler are the double taper floating line and the weight forward medium sinking line. The line sizes are AFTM 4 to 9 for trout – larger size fly lines are used for salmon. To identify the type of line when buying is fairly easy. For an example, the double taper floating line is labelled as DTF plus its AFTM size, and the forward taper sinker is WFS. Double taper lines have the taper at both ends of the fly line. When one end becomes worn and tacky, it is an easy matter to reverse the line on the reel and use the other end. Forward taper lines, or if you prefer, the weight forward line, consist of a single taper which is followed by the running line or shooting line. This line is designed for longer distance casting than the double taper. To cast the forward taper, it is necessary to get the taper portion of the line in the air by false casting. When there is enough line in the air and the line speed is correct, on the forward cast let it go and shoot it out – thus presenting the fly. Although it is not possible to achieve distance quite so easily with the double taper it makes it possible to present the fly much more gently and accurately.

For general fly-fishing you can use the double taper and the weight forward – both sinkers and floaters are more than adequate for most applications. The sinking lines are available in slow sink, medium sink, fast sink and very fast sink.

There are double taper sink tip lines which are basically a floating line with a sinking tip of three or four metres. These are very useful for river fishing particularly in the fast runs where it is necessary to get the fly down to the fish quickly. Finally, for the angler who requires distance for their fishing, there is the shooting head. This is a heavy fly line of 9 m (30 ft) attached to a nylon line backing, which when used with the double-haul casting technique enables fantastic distances to be achieved – thereby reaching water that is normally out of range.

## Fly Rods

Most fly rods are manufactured from carbon fibre, glass fibre or cane. The range of rods available should more than cover most angler's needs. Dealing only with fly rods designed for trout fishing, these are available in lengths from six feet (1·80 m) to eleven feet (3·30 m). Their action will depend on which material is used for their manufacture. Carbon fibre rods are light and easy to handle and can be used all day long without too much fatigue, so they are suitable for the older or disabled angler. Carbon glass fibre rods are also very light when compared with the fly rods of a few years ago. They have a wide range of action and apart from some up-market models their prices are reasonable. This rod would probably be the ideal choice for the casual fly-fisher who only requires one rod which is capable of presenting a 'fly', ranging from small dry flies to medium lures, to the fish.

Finally the cane rod, the rod of the connoisseur. The split cane rod has across its range a unique and distinctive action which makes it a joy to use. The action is in its whole length, from butt to tip, and in the hands of an expert its accuracy and presentation is second to none. In the longer lengths of cane rod and cane rods designed to handle the heavier fly lines, its weight may not endear it to the older anglers who are perhaps feeling their years. For the younger fly-fisher who can handle it, the cane rod is a rod that must be tried, particularly for river fishing.

The line sizes are given for each model by the rod manufacturers using the AFTM code for each rod. Usually most good quality fly rods can be used quite comfortably using fly lines one size heavier or lighter than the designed size.

I would suggest to the newcomer to fly-fishing that before he goes out and spends a lot of money kitting himself up, he first finds an experienced person to advise him. If this is not possible, visit as many tackle shops as you can, listen to what they have to say and have a good look around at the tackle on offer. Go home with the literature of the tackle being offered and study it thoroughly. You will be spoiled for choice but do not rush your decision. Of the tackle shop personnel who have offered you advice, try to separate the fisherman salesperson from the high pressure salesperson pushing for sales, probably for the higher priced items.

Fishing tackle manufacturers in the United Kingdom all produce excellent quality flyrods throughout their range at prices which are reasonable and competitive. I do not propose to stick my neck out and make any recommendations. All I will suggest is initially the choice of fly rod should be of glass carbon or carbon if you can afford it. This rod should be capable of presenting small dry flies accurately and gently if handled correctly, also have enough power to handle a team of wet flies and longshank lures. It should have the AFTM rating of size six to size eight fly lines.

When using only one fly rod I will always use the forward taper a size heavier than the double taper. This is because it is possible to load the rod heavier when casting with a double taper line than with the single taper or if you prefer to call it, weight forward line.

To be able to cover all the conditions and types of water met in a day's fly-fishing it is a good idea to have three different types of fly lines each on their own spools or reels. The reels should be large enough to accommodate at least seventy metres of nylon backing line, twenty-five pounds (11·35 kg) breaking strain and of course the fly line. Ideally the reel should be of 1:2 gearing and have the capability of quick change spare spools for the different fly lines.

The ideal outfit for the beginner is a flyrod of nine feet (2·70 m) long, rated fly line sizes AFTM 6 or 8, a geared fly reel with three spools, each spool loaded with three different fly lines plus backing. The fly lines should be DTF6 (Double Taper Floater size 6), WFS7 (Weight Forward Sinker size 7) and DTST6 (Double Taper Sink Tip size 6). Also needed is an appropriate selection of flies and accessories, casts, scissors, pliers, creel or fishing bag and landing net. This should equip the beginner with all that is necessary to cover the range of trout fishing. I am assuming the basics of handling the fly rod have already been mastered.

Landing nets are very important and this is an area where, perhaps, not quite enough attention is given for the novice. Folding nets are very convenient to carry on the belt while fishing up the river bank. However problems do arise when moving through undergrowth; the loose end of the net always manage to snag and get caught on brambles, twigs and barbed wire. Quite often when the time comes to flick the net open to land a fish, the net develops a mind of its own. It makes interesting fishing trying, at the same time, to keep control of a fish, prepare the net for landing it and being careful not to drop the rod point – thereby giving the fish slack line which may in turn allow it to slip the hook. No, folding nets are not for me. I always use the type where the handle is telescopic or the gye type, where the handle can be closed by pushing it across the face of the net ring, and extended when required for use. Personally I always have my net ready before I start fishing. When walking up the bank between fishing stands it is no problem to push the handle in, to reduce its length and open it again at the next stand. Always make sure the net is of adequate size for the fish you are likely to catch. It is better to have the net too large than one that is too small. This lesson was very clearly impressed on me many years ago when I lost a fresh run grilse by trying to stuff it into a too small flick-up trout net.

As the angler gains experience his equipment needs may change. Instead of having different lines on spare spools to increase his capabilities, he should consider having additional fly rods to perform the different applications for the various modes. For dry fly-fishing the rod will have to be capable of casting very light double taper floating line size 4 or 5. When fishing with a team of wet flies or loch style boat fishing, the rod needs to be stiffer in action and longer, rated for AFTM fly line sizes 6 or 7. Casting the fly-lures needs a very powerful rod capable of handling the heavy fly lines and shooting heads. For this mode of fly-fishing for trout the rods can be up to eleven feet (3·30m) in length and able to handle fly lines and shooting heads up to AFTM size eleven.

On arrival at the water's edge, always spend some time in observation. A few minutes spent in studying the prevailing conditions before tackling up is never wasted time. On stillwaters the water conditions are often a good indicator of which fishing method may be suitable. If the water surface is flat calm or there is just a slight ripple this is ideal perhaps for nymph or dry fly-fishing – particularly if there are a few daytime sedges flittering out over the water or perhaps the longhorns are swarming in the margins. When the wind has created a good ripple in the lake's surface, wind slicks will sometimes form. The slicks are flat calms of water running through the ripple like a road through the countryside. In the calm water of these slicks all sorts of trout food items will gather and be held. The trout will cruise usually upwind in these slicks, feeding. They are relatively easy to spot as they travel up the slick nose and tailing along taking food here and there. Good fishing can be had if the slick is close enough to be reached from the shore or by drifting a boat nearby and fishing a team of wet flies across it. Should there be a strong wind blowing across the lake pushing up a big wave, this is the time for sinking lines and lure fishing. Move into a position where the wind does not make casting too difficult and cast the lure out on the sinking line; give it time to sink, then fish it back.

For lake fishing my equipment is rather modest. I use a 8½ foot (2·60 m) long carbon fibre rod rated AFTM 6 to 8 lines sizes and two gearfly reels with two spare spools. The fly lines are Double Taper Floating size six, Weight Forward size seven sinking, Double Taper Sink Tip size six and Shooting Head Sinker size eight. I also have a 9½ foot (2·85 m) glass fibre rod which I use for upstream nymph/spider fishing in fast waters with a sink-tip double taper size six line. For brook fly-fishing I have a seven (2·10 m) foot glass fibre rod which I use with DTF4 very successfully. The very light size four floating line is ideal for fishing nymphs and dry flies in these little brooks for the small wild brown that can take and eject a fly quicker than it takes to blink. Using this outfit on small private lakes I have hooked and beaten rainbow trout of over five pounds (2·27 kg) with a three pound (1·36 kg) breaking strain point. I do not think I would care to try a big fish on this tackle in a river in high water conditions.

# 9

# Fly Lure Tying Techniques

This chapter is for the benefit of those readers who have no experience of fly-tying. In previous chapters I have touched upon fly-tying techniques when constructing in part or in full some of the spinning lures. To assist the reader to understand this better (and the following fly lure chapters), I am giving some details of tying techniques, materials and tools required, but it is by no means a complete list. Although it is possible to tie flies holding the hook in the fingers, the only tool used being a sharp pair of scissors, I would suggest the following tools are acquired which will make the tying operation considerably easier.

One fly-tying vice
Good quality scissors
Hackle pliers
Dubbing needle
Razor blade
Bobbin holder

The vice should be of the type where the jaws can be rotated, thus allowing the fly to be observed in each tying stage.

How to tie a hacklewing lure is illustrated by the following instructions for dressing the Black Streamer. Place the hook in the vice and tighten, making sure the hook is secure and will not move about during the dressing process. Whip a bed of silk up the hookshank; take a bunch of cock hackle fibres from a saddle hackle and tie in to form the tail. Now tie in a length of wool and gold oval tinsel. Wind the black wool up the hookshank forming the body and then rib with gold oval tinsel. Secure the wool and tinsel ends, cutting off the surplus. Prepare a black cock hackle and tie in and wind. Sweeping the hackle back so to veil the body, prepare a good silk foundation for the hackle wing. Select four cock hackles from the cape for the wing. Prepare and measure them for size, and when satisfied, tie them in with the hackle points looking out over the hookeye. Trim off the hackle stalks and double the hackles back and overtie, thus forming the streamer wing. Complete the silk head and whip finish. After giving the fly head a couple coats of varnish the streamer is now complete and ready for use.

## Whip finish knot

The finishing off process for a fly's head is most important and the three turn whip finish is the best. To apply the whip after completing the fly head, first make a loop of silk. This loop should be made so that it is hanging below the fly and the bobbin holder end is laid against the hookshank, looking back to the bend. Take the bottom of the loop and twist it so that it traps the bobbin holder silk end against the hookshank where the head of fly is. Do this three times, keeping firm pressure

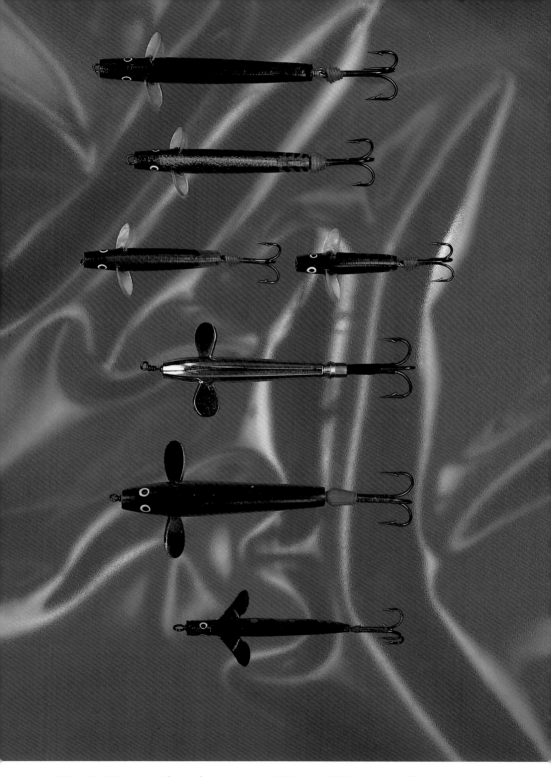

*Plate* 7  Minnows (*from the top*): Lane Minnow 2³/₄ in (approx. 7 cm); Lane Minnow 2¹/₄ in (approx. 6 cm); Lane Minnow 1¹/₂ in (approx. 4 cm); Lane Minnow 1¹/₄ in (approx. 3 cm); Dexter Silver Devon Minnow; Standard Yellow Belly Devon; Quill Minnow. *Photo: Gordon Bellman*

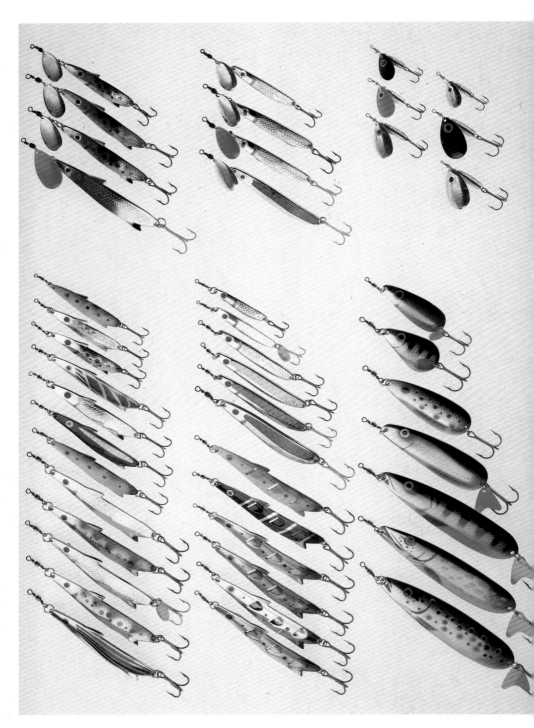

*Plate 8* Landa Lures (*first row, from the top*) 1–4 Lukki + FlipZ, 5–16 Lukki
Lures; (*middle row, from the top*) 1–4 Herri + FlipZ, 5–10 Herri Lures, 11–16
Lukki Lures; (*third row, from the top*) 1–6 FlipZ Bar-spinners, 7–8 Pikko Fatta
Spoons, 9–10 Pikko Thina Spoons, 11–13 Pikko Longa Spoons.
*Photo: Courtesy Landa Sport Ltd*

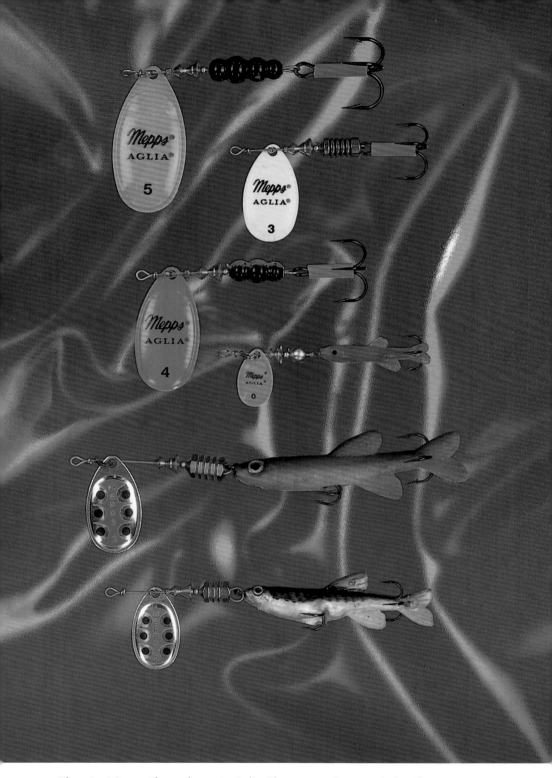

*Plate 9* Mepps (*from the top*): Aglia Fluorescent Orange; Aglia Fluorescent Chartreuse; Aglia Fluorescent Rose; Orange Mini Saumon; Gold TW – Rouge; Silver TW – Mino Natural. *Photo: Gordon Bellman*

*Plate 10*  Delta, Assorted Flasha Spoons (*from the top*): Green; Red; Chartreuse;
Brown; Blue. *Photo: Gordon Bellman*

on the loop. Place the point of scissors or a dubbing needle in the loop, making sure the tension is not relaxed. Catch hold of the bobbin and pull the loop closed, still keeping the pressure on to avoid the silk turns from slipping. When the loop has pulled the dubbing needle close to the fly head, slip it out and pull the loop through the three turns of silk. The whip finish knot is now complete; after varnishing the fly should never unwind and this is the difference between a quality fly and the other types.

## Hair Wing Lures

Tie the body, tail and hackle as already described for the Black Streamer. Now take a bunch of hair from a tail and tie in on top of the hookshank, then trim off the surplus hair looking out from hookshank at an angle. Work plenty of varnish into the cut ends to cement them in. Complete the head with turns of silk. Cutting off the surplus hair at an angle allows a nice tapered head to be formed. Now varnish and leave to dry and then varnish again to achieve a quality finish.

When dressing a multi-colour hair wing I like to tie the colours in separately – it gives the wing more 'life' in the whole effect than a wing where the hair has been dressed in one operation. I dress my wing by adding the colours on top of each other. When I add the next bunch of hair on top of the turns of silk, I make sure the first two turns of silk are directly on top of the turns of silk below; the third turn I take behind them, thus pulling the bunch of hair directly down on the different coloured hair below it; I use the loop over the top technique – the same method as for tying a feathered wing. I continue adding the different coloured layers of hair until the full colour wing is completed, trim the surplus hair off at an angle and finish as previously described. This technique of dressing multi-colour wings can bulk up the head if too many turns of silk are used, but with practice it is surprising how well the hair will stay in position with only one or two turns of silk during the tying operation. The pattern that requires the hairwing to encircle the body can be dressed by two methods; firstly this can be achieved by tying little bunches of hair around the hookshank; the other technique is to take a large bunch of hair, secure loosely on the hookshank with a couple of turns of silk and spread the hair with finger and thumb. With a little practice you will find that this is probably the best technique.

## Tubes Flies

These are dressed on brass or plastic tubes which are slid onto the cast and then a treble hook is tied on. With the smaller tubes, where the hookeye will not fit inside the tube, a small piece of bicycle valve rubber must be fixed over its end so that the treble hook can be held in line with the tube. There are tubes which are specially manufactured for fly-tying which have a cavity in the tail to take the eye of the treble hook so that it is always in perfect alignment.

No special tools are required to dress tube flies, just some salmon hooks of various sizes with their loop eyes removed. To dress a tube fly, place the eyeless salmon hook into the vice and tighten. Slip the tube on to the eyeless hook, pressing it on firmly. It is very important that the tube is properly seated on the hookshank; should it become loose and spin around during the tying operation you will have to start again. Wind the silk down the tube and tie in the body and ribbing material – then complete the body. Ensure there is a good silk layer for the foundation of the wing; animal hair just whipped on a bare base will not stay in position long. Take the hair in small batches from the tail, rotating the tube on the hookshank for tying each bunch. Trim off surplus hair from each batch before tying on the next; this avoids the tyer having his view obscured by splayed out ends of surplus hair during the following stages. Repeat this process until the whole circumference of the tube is covered. Tidy up the loose ends and give the head and cut hair ends a good coat of varnish. Complete the head and whip finish, followed by another coat of varnish when dry. Some patterns may require a hackle in front of the wing; tie this hackle in and wind so that it forms a collar, sweep back and overtie to form a neat head to the dressing. To improve the appearance of the tube I dress the treble hooks with a brightly dyed cock hackle which is tied in close to the hookeye and partly swept back. I consider this improves the 'taking' qualities of the tube fly.

## Tandem Two Hook Mounts

Place what is going to be the rear hook in the vice. Prepare a bed of silk down the hookshank. Take a piece of nylon monofilament of 10 lb (4·54 kg) breaking strain, lay it onto the hookshank and whip it on from eye to bend, doubling the nylon back so that it is again back on top of the hookshank and whip back from the bend to the eye and secure. You will now have a hook with two pieces of nylon line 4 in (10 cm) long sticking out over the hookeye. Varnish the whipping and leave to dry. It is a good idea to prepare a dozen or so rear hooks at a time. When the varnish is dry, complete the body dressing of the rear hook of the tandem mount in the vice. Place the front hook of the tandem mount in the vice, whip on a bed of silk, take the completed rear hook and lay the nylon line which is already tied into the rear hook on to the front hookshank. Secure with a few turns of silk; check the distance between the two hooks, making sure the gap is not so wide that when the lure is completed and in use the rear hook cannot catch up in the front hook. Satisfied that the distance is right, complete whipping on the nylon line from bend to eye. Doubling the nylon line back, whip down back to the hook bend, cut off the surplus nylon line and whip the silk back to the eye and whip finish. Varnish the whipping. When the varnish is dry, complete the tandem hooklure with what ever pattern is decided.

The same principles apply to the three or four hook mounts and flying treble. Instead of dressing a body on the flying treble I always use a bright red, green, orange or yellow silk for the whipping and just varnish it; sometimes I will use gold or silver tinsel on the treble hook to give the fly a little bit of flash. A tandem lure so constructed is virtually indestructible within the breaking strain of the double nylon line.

## Deer Hair Heads

Deer hair is very buoyant owing to its hollow structure and insulating properties. Bushy flies dressed with deer hair are virtually unsinkable; probably only cork bodied flies are better.

To dress deer hair heads or bodies requires a different technique to any other tying operation, this is known as spinning the deer hair. It has to be done on the bare hookshank; when dressing a muddler type lure you have to leave enough room (bare hookshank) aftér completing the body and wing. Coat the bare hookshank on which you are going to spin the deer hair head with varnish. Cut a bunch of deer hair off the skin and lay it on the hookshank with the fine points looking toward the hookbend. Take two loose turns over the deer hair, adjusting it to allow for whatever hackle length is required. Tighten the silk firmly, at the same time leaving go the deer hair which was being held on top of the hookshank. Because the deer hair is hollow this technique will cause the hair to spin around the bare hookshank and at the same time flare out like an umbrella being opened. Continue taking bunches of deer hair and repeating this process, varnishing the hookshank between each spinning. When the spinning of deer hair is complete, finish off with a three turn whip finish and repeat the three turn whip – varnish liberally and leave to dry. When the varnish has set trim to a neat tadpole shape, leaving the fine points of the first spinning pointing towards the hook bend as the hackle. For big bulky heads which do not require much trimming use a small naked flame and lightly singe the deer hair to achieve the shape required.

## Marabou
Marabou feathers are from the underside of a turkey. They are a very soft and mobile feather and the fibres, because of their mobility, will impart 'life' to a fly which is just cast out and allowed to sink; the downward movement in the water will cause the fly to work. Marabou fibres are great favourites for winging and tails of lures.

## Lead Heads
Lead head lures in recent times have become very popular. It is not a new idea – I think it was Trevor Housby who popularized this idea in his book many years ago. With the influx of new materials and fly-tyers this mode has been developed further. Partridge Hooks have developed a special hook for this mode from a Trevor Housby design. Its code number is K9A.

To dress the lead head lure, first glue or whip the metal head into place close up to the hookeye. Whip the silk down the hookshank; tie the tail in to place, add body materials and wind; tie in and wind the hackle close to the metal bead, sweeping the hackle fibres back so that they veil the body, and overtie. After tying in the marabou wing, whip finish and varnish including the metal bead. The metal bead can be varnished or painted any colour. It may be necessary to give the head two or three coats of paint or varnish to ensure a quality finish. The lure is now ready to be used but when first casting a weighted fly of this type, you will find it a bit tricky. It will be necessary to slow your action and line speed down. There are special adaptions for lead head flies available including Barbell types of weight which can be tied close to the hookshank to give the lure weight also to simulate eyes which can be painted the appropriate colour.

## Class or Metal Beads
For years I have used this method to tie beads into fly patterns; it is very durable and suitable for any type of bead no matter what the construction material, providing it has a hole in the middle. My method of constructing, or rather tying

in beads is very easy. It is a good way of using beads to simulate the eyes of the various underwater creatures, and in the case of the metal beads it adds the necessary weight for the leadhead design.

Tie your fly in the normal manner, taking care to make the head a little longer than usual. Now take two beads and a short piece of nylon monofilament (the size of the beads and the breaking strain of nylon monofilament are the tyer's choice – depending on the size of the fly or lure being tied). Thread the beads onto the nylon line and tie in the nylon close to the hookeye, with the beads on a loop lying over the fly body. Firmly pull the loose ends of the nylon until the beads are sitting snugly on the hookshank between the hackle and hookeye. Press down on the beads with your thumb until they are lying each side of the hookshank, then double the nylon line back so that it is lying on the fly body. Making sure that the nylon has passed between the beads on top of the hookshank, secure it with a few turns of silk. Now slowly pull the nylon line ends toward the bend and at the same time press down on the beads with the thumb; this will force the beads even further onto the sides of the hookshank. Keeping pressure on the nylon line so that it does not slip back, take a few more turns of silk between the beads and hackle, then secure the beads with figure of eight turns of silk. Cut off any surplus nylon and whip finish. Varnish liberally thus ensuring that the head and eyes are virtually indestructible. To impart additional life to the fly, tie peacock or ostrich herl between the hackle and beads; this, when wound, gives a bulky head.

## Delta Tackle (UK): Delta Tails

The Delta tail story is quite interesting. It started in 1970 in Plymouth, Devon, England – when Henry McConnell opened a shop selling tropical fish. After a couple of years he started to stock and sell various pieces of fishing equipment to the local anglers which proved to be a great success.

Spending long hours in the shop he had the time to study the fish and their behaviour. He noticed that if a fish was unwell for some reason, its swimming pattern would change. It would swim to the surface, hang there for a few seconds and then slowly sink for a while, then recover and swim to the surface again. Henry noticed that this behaviour would alert some of the bigger fish in the tank. If he was not quick enough getting the distressed fish out of the tank, the others soon attacked it. This gave him the idea of developing a lure that could be fished in such a manner. In 1978 he started manufacturing fishing tackle and it was at this time he developed his high density polystyrene float and the first mini plastic eels.

It was in the late seventies that I noticed the plastic eels in tackleshops in Plymouth. I incorporated some of the tail ends of these plastic eels into experimental fly patterns. However I was not the only one to try this: an article duly appeared in the angling press giving details of the new mode of tying and using the Delta plastic eels in fly dressing. The lures in the article were designed for 10–13 cm (4–5 in) lures and were for deep fishing for big brown trout in reservoirs. The flies in which I incorporated the plastic Delta eel were sea trout flies. I did not use the whole eel, just the tail section, tying them in as an ordinary tail is tied in. These flies proved to be very successful in my mode for sea trout; the mode given in the article used the whole artificial Delta eel.

Henry McConnell soon realised the significances of this and in 1981 produced

Delta fly tails especially for flies in the following colours: red, white, fluorescent yellow, fluorescent orange, fluorescent green, nymph brown, black and luminescent. Delta Tackle have now outgrown their premises and are to be found at their new premises on the Parkway industrial estate on the outskirts of Plymouth. The bulk of their business is supplying tackle for sea fishing.

Using the Delta fly tail in fly-tying is very easy because its design makes it so. To place the tail on the hookshank can be done in two ways: either slip it on through the hole at the end of fly body by passing the hookeye into it or place the front body hole over the hook barb and thread the fly tail on. Before placing the fly tail on the hook shank, put on a spot of glue to secure it. Now slide the tail on to the hookshank, taking care not to let the tail start following the bend of the hook. This is most important; the tail body should be on the hookshank and the tail should be perfectly in line with the hookshank. If the tail is not glued properly on the shank, it will not swim properly. After making sure all is in line I always put a spot of glue in the hole under the tail where the hookshank comes out before the bend.

Fish the flies that are dressed with the fly tail with a sink and draw, then pause, technique. This will reproduce the action of the sick fish as originally observed by Henry McConnell in his shop. Using a floating line and move the fly in long steady pulls on the fly line. This will cause the plastic fly tail to wriggle most enticingly. The takes will mostly come when the fly stops and starts to sink.

# 10

# Fly Lures

The fly lure has always been an important addition to the fly-fisher's repertoire. In the UK the fly lure has been used on freshwater lakes and lochs since the last century.

For the first fifty years or so of the twentieth century the British angler tended to fish the traditional lure patterns which were mostly dressings from the turn of the century. Very little progress (apart from the odd new dressing) was made regarding fly lures for stillwaters, but for salmon and trout flies the changes in their dressings and new patterns has always been an ongoing process.

Because of the availability of more stillwaters for fly-fishing and leisure time, lure fishing has developed at a tremendous rate in the second part of the twentieth century. With such a vast influx of new thinking, not bound by the chains of tradition, it was no surprise that there were many new innovations in fly design and fishing techniques. More fly-fishermen learned to tie their own flies, creating in turn an explosion of fly patterns, many of which have stood the test of time. For many of the new dressings the longshank hook became a firm favourite, particularly for streamers and minnow-imitating lures.

The streamer fly has always been a firm favourite with the North American fly-fisher and the first patterns used in the UK came from American tyers. This is no longer the case as there are now plenty of British designs available for the fly-fisher.

It is pleasing to see the multi hook and tandem lures becoming fashionable again. There are many configurations for the hook in the tandem or multi hook mount. The most normal practice for the tandem is two hooks with their hook points downwards. A variation on this can be the rear hook having its barb upwards and masked by the lure's wing. This type of construction can be done with the three or four multi hook mounts. Triangle and double hooks can be used as well as the single hook, longshank or normal shank hook. It is the tyer's choice.

Hardy Bros, at the end of the last century, produced some useful tandem and multi hook lures for game fish in their own fly-tying department. These were largely used in the freshwater lochs and estuaries; they were very popular at the turn of the century on the estuaries of the Dee, Don, Ythan, Deveron, Ugie, Ness and the Kyles of Sutherland and Tongue.

## Hardy Bros: Multi and Tandem Lures 1894

### Dandy
*Body*  Oval silver tinsel size 18, both hooks
*Hackle*  Dyed red long fibre cock
*Wing*  Strips from grey mallard flank
*Head*  Black varnish

The length of this lure is restricted by the mallard grey flank feather length. For longer wings change to grizzle cock hackles.

### Blue Terror
*Tail*   Red wool, both hooks
*Body*   Oval silver tinsel size 18, both hooks
*Wing*   Two dyed blue hackles flanked two-thirds of its length with strips of grey mallard flank feather
*Head*   Black varnish

### Black Terror
*Body*   Black wool ribbed silver tinsel, both hooks
*Wing*   Black hackles over and under hookshank
*Head*   Black varnish

The black cock hackles are dressed as two wings. One wing over the hookshank as normal, the other wing under the hookshank, its length to match the wing above it. Each wing consists of two black hackles, back to back.

### Demon
*Tail*   Red wool
*Body*   Silver oval tinsel, both hooks
*Hackle*   Dyed red cock
*Wing*   Badger cock hackles
*Head*   Black varnish

### Peacock Eye Demon
*Tail*   Red wool
*Body*   Silver oval tinsel, both hooks
*Hackle*   Dyed blue or blue peacock hackle
*Wings*   Herls from peacock eye feather
*Head*   Black varnish

For this lure select the herl from the peacock eye feather which has a natural curve to it. Tie it in, taking advantage of this curve so that the herl will taper nicely over the rear hook, thereby giving the wing a good shape which in turns shows off the quality of the dressing.

### Worm Fly
*Body*   Peacock herl, both hooks
*Hackle*   Furnace cock, both hooks
*Head*   Black varnish

Both hooks on this tandem lure must be finished off with long fibre cock hackles. The modern dressing of the wormfly has red wool tags.

All the above lures can be dressed with any hook size, longshank or normal wide gape.

The following two hook lures I designed for sea trout and lake trout in the early sixties. They are useful for fishing for sea trout during the day on fast sinking lines with short leaders. This technique can be very effective particularly if there is a tinge of colour in the water. The sea trout usually takes the lure as the line curves across the current and speeds the fly up. For slow flowing or deep pools it will be necessary to speed the lure up by hand, stripping and making the fly work: this is a good technique for taking the occasional salmon if there is one in the pool. These lures work well for freshrun fish, the sea trout will really chop them, especially in the lower reaches of the river where they have just come out of the saltwater.

### Silvery Grey Lure
*Tail*   D.F.M. orange wool
*Body*   Silver tinsel ribbed silver oval
*Hackle*   Long-fibred golden pheasant red breast feather
*Wing*   Grey mallard flank
*Cheeks*   Jungle cock or substitute

### Silver Blue Lure
*Tail*   Red wool
*Body*   Silver tinsel ribbed silver oval
*Hackle*   Long fibred blue peacock hackle
*Wing*   Grey mallard dyed blue
*Cheeks*   Jungle cock or substitute

### Claret and Mallard
*Tail*   Magenta wool
*Body*   Dark claret seal's fur ribbed gold oval
*Hackle*   Golden pheasant red breast
*Wing*   Brown mallard

### Silver Ghost Lure
*Tail*   White D.F.M. wool
*Body*   Silver tinsel ribbed silver oval
*Hackle*   White cock
*Wing*   Grey mallard flank
*Cheeks*   Red wool clipped short

### Alexandra
*Tail*   Dyed red goose
*Body*   Silver tinsel ribbed silver oval
*Hackle*   Blue peacock
*Wing*   Peacock sword feather
*Sides*   Dyed red goose
*Cheeks*   Jungle cock

### Dunkeld Lure
*Tail*   Yellow D.F.M. wool
*Body*   Gold tinsel ribbed gold oval
*Hackle*   Dyed hot orange
*Wing*   Brown mallard
*Cheeks*   Jungle cock

### Butcher Lure
*Tail*   Red wool
*Body*   Silver tinsel ribbed silver oval
*Hackle*   Dyed red cock
*Wing*   Black squirrel

*Hook sizes*: wide gape six or eight or combination of the two sizes with the size eight at the rear.

The next lure I designed in the mid-eighties using what was then a new plastic tinsel material called Flashabou.

### Dirty Water Lure
*Hook*   Size 6
*Tail*   Hot orange cock fibres
*Body*   Red wool ribbed silver oval
*Hackle*   Hot orange cock
*Wing*   Flashabou, red-blue-silver mixed

The uses for plastic tinsel material in fly-tying is endless and I expect usage of these and other new materials to increase as time moves on because of their ease of application and the shortage of traditional materials.

The next series of lures are designed for trolling in lakes and lochs. Most big brown trout in this type of water will not normally come to the traditional fly patterns and techniques except, perhaps, at mayfly time. It is necessary to fish for them trolling outsize multi-hook lures. The lures should be 10–15 cm (4–6 in) long. It is the size of the lure which will attract these trout, as a considerable portion of their diet consists of small fish and this mode of fishing is probably the only hope of taking these trout. During the day they stay out in deep water and are very seldom found close to the shore, except in autumn when they will congregate around the feeder streams prior to spawning. After it becomes dark these big fish will move in close to the shore to feed. Even where the fishery rules allows fishing one hour after sunset, these trout are difficult to take on ordinary lures. I suspect the really wary big trout do not come into the shallows to feed until very much later. Only by trolling the deeper water well off-shore with these big lures on fast sinking or lead core fly lines will the angler have any chance of getting on terms, during the day, with these big and very wary cannibal trout.

### Blue Devil
*Tail*   White marabou fibres
*Body*   Gold tinsel ribbed gold oval
*Hackles*   All hooks white long fibre cock
*Wings*   Six grizzle saddle hackles dyed blue
*Cheeks*   Blue peacock neck

### Yellow Devil
*Tail*   Yellow marabou fibres
*Body*   Gold tinsel ribbed oval
*Hackle*   Dyed yellow bucktail
*Wing*   Brown bucktail dyed yellow
*Cheeks*   Dyed red goose strips

### White Peril
*Tail*   White marabou fibres
*Body*   Silver tinsel ribbed oval
*Hackle*   White marabou fibres
*Wings*   White marabou with brown bucktail over
*Cheeks*   Red goose strips

**Orange Peril**
*Tail*   Orange and green marabou fibres
*Body*   Gold tinsel ribbed oval
*Hackle*   Green marabou fibres
*Wing*   Orange marabou with dyed orange bucktail over

**Red Peril**
*Tail*   Red and white marabou
*Body*   Silver tinsel ribbed oval
*Hackle*   White marabou fibres
*Wings*   Red marabou with brown bucktail over

*Hook sizes* and number of hooks used to make the mounts are the tyer's choice.

## Plastic Fly Tail Lures
I have designed the following lures using Henry McConnell Delta plastic fly tails. These plastic fly tails can be dressed on single hooks mainly in the following sizes: 4, 6, 8 and 10. There are two sizes of fly tails in the colours available, large or small.

**Black/Orange**
*Tail/Body*   Black fly tail, large
*Thorax*   Orange wool
*Hackle*   Black
*Wing*   Black cock hackles

**Hot Orange**
*Tail/Body*   Orange fly tail, large
*Thorax*   Magenta wool
*Hackle*   Orange
*Wing*   Orange cock hackles

**Yellow Lure**
*Tail/Body*   Yellow fly tail, large
*Thorax*   Yellow wool
*Hackle*   Yellow
*Wing*   Cree cock hackles dyed yellow

**Green Lure**
*Tail/Body*   Green fly tail, large
*Thorax*   Green wool
*Hackle*   Grizzle dyed green
*Wing*   Grizzle cock dyed green

**White Lure**
*Tail/Body*   White fly tail, large
*Thorax*   Red wool
*Hackle*   White cock
*Wing*   White marabou, grey squirrel over

**Tadpole**
*Tail/Body*   Black fly tail, small
*Hackle*   Black cock

*Head*   Black chenille
*Hook*   Longshank size eight

To dress the tadpole, first glue a plastic fly tail on the hookshank. Tie in a black cock hackle close to the eye. Wind the hackle and sweep it back to veil the body and overtie. Finish off with black chenille to form a large bulky head.

### White Wiggler
*Tail/Body*   White fly tail
*Hackle*   Grey partridge, swept back to veil body
*Head*   White chenille

### Damsel Wiggler
*Tail/Body*   Green fly tail
*Hackle*   Grey partridge, swept back to veil body
*Head*   Peacock herl

### Orange Wiggler
*Tail/Body*   Orange fly tail
*Hackle*   Brown partridge, swept back to veil body
*Head*   Brown chenille

### Yellow Wiggler
*Tail/Body*   Yellow fly tail
*Hackle*   Grey partridge, swept back to veil body
*Head*   Peacock herl

### Bloodworm
*Tail/Body*   Red fly tail
*Hackle*   Scarlet cock, swept back to veil body
*Head*   Dyed red ostrich herl

Dress the wigglers on size six or eight wide gape hooks, small tails and the bloodworm on a size eight hook with a few turns of copper wire under the ostrich herl. This will make it sink quicker and give it the correct movement when fishing it sink and draw.

### Stick Fly
*Tail/Body*   Brown fly tail
*Thorax*   Yellow wool
*Hackle*   Furnace cock swept back veiling body
*Silk*   Red
*Hook*   Longshank size 8 or 6

The stick fly should be fished very slowly near the lake's bed, sometimes letting it rest on the bottom for a while and then lifting it off and retrieving again. This tactic will induce the fish which have been following to take most times; the take, when it comes, can be quite vicious. This tactic will also work with the bloodworm and wigglers. The wigglers are designed to be a general representation of the various types of aquatic life-forms that inhabit our stillwaters. The range of colour in the same species of underwater creatures can vary quite considerably, therefore choice of colour can be a very important factor if you are to be successful. Time spent observing the water and fly-life before fishing is never time wasted. If there are fish fry in the shallows the white wiggler can be a good choice of pattern. When there are plenty of dragonflies bobbing over the water, the damsel wiggler may prove to be a suitable choice.

**Sedge Pupa**
*Tail/Body*   Orange fly tail
*Hackle*   Woodcock swept back over body
*Head*   Peacock herl

**Claret Pupa**
*Tail/Body*   Red fly tail
*Hackle*   Cock hackle dyed claret
*Head*   Ostrich herl dyed claret

**Green Pupa**
*Tail/Body*   Green fly tail
*Hackle*   Woodcock swept back over body
*Head*   Peacock herl

**Yellow Pupa**
*Tail/Body*   Yellow fly tail
*Hackle*   Yellow cock
*Head*   Ostrich herl dyed brown

**Black Pupa**
*Tail/Body*   Black fly tail
*Hackle*   Red cock
*Head*   Black ostrich herl

The pupa series are intended to represent the various colours of the sedge pupa generally. For best results they should be fished with floating lines and long leaders on the lakes. On the rivers the sink-tip fly line and short leaders would be more suitable, particularly if the river is fast flowing. The claret pupa is very effective for wild brown trout in high lakes and lochs. Hook size should be size eight wide gape only.

The normally dressed baby doll lure is a very efficient taker of trout. I have dressed a series of baby dolls incorporating the flytail instead of the normal wool tail and back. For the body I use long fibred chenille with a false hackle of cock hackle fibres and the head finished off with two large white beads for eyes.

**White Baby Doll**
*Tail*   White fly tail
*Body*   White chenille
*Hackle*   Dyed red cock

**Yellow Baby Doll**
*Tail*   Yellow fly tail
*Body*   Yellow chenille
*Hackle*   Dyed yellow cock

The white and yellow versions I found to be most effective followed closely by the orange. For the doll's dressing, any colour combinations can be used, depending on the requirement and waters to be fished.

Stickleback fry, where they occur, provide a useful food item for some stillwaters. In the summer these small fish usually congregate in shoals in the margins of lakes and it is at this time that the trout become preoccupied with the abundance of food. I have been on the banks of lakes when the water only a short distance out erupts with small fish trying to escape the trout, which hang about out in the deeper water and make regular forays into the margins. When this happens, tie on the stickleback lure and when the trout makes its next run into the shallows try to present and fish the lure in front of him. The opportunity to do this does not arise very often and the only other method is to cast the artificial out into the deeper water and draw it into the shallows in an attractive manner; pause for a moment after fishing out a cast before lifting off and casting again. Fish will often seize the lure just as it breaks the surface of the water. When this happens the fish hits it in such an explosive manner that the hard take and the splash that follows always gives one quite a start, no matter how prepared you are. When fishing a fry imitation it is important to mount an artificial which corresponds nearest to the natural fry in the water at the time; the angler who copies the actions of the natural will, if size and colour is right, always take fish.

### Stickleback
*Tail*   Green wool or fly tail
*Body*   Silver tinsel, thorax red wool
*Overbody*   Clear PVC
*Hackle*   Olive cock
*Head*   Peacock herl
*Hook*   Longshank size 6 or 8

To tie the stickleback, first secure the tail on the hookshank; tie in silver tinsel and form the under body; the red wool thorax can now be tied in and formed. Cut the PVC into narrow strips, tie them in and wind to form the body. As you wind keep a firm pressure on it and gently stretch it; this will give a very neat tight translucent body. After winding the plastic strips into a fish-shaped body, tie in the olive hackle and wind. Finish off with a peacock herl head. The lure should now look like a small fish with the silver and red underbody being visible through the plastic translucent overbody.

The first time I used plastic tails in flies was many years ago. These tails were cut down plastic mini sand eels which were originally manufactured for sea fishing. I tied these tails into standard sea trout fly patterns and with the help of friends tried them out with very good results. Since then I have tied the plastic eel tail and the plastic fly tail into many new and standard fly patterns for lake or sea trout fishing; in some cases the standard patterns have become much more effective. One of my favourite modes of tying is the 'Killer' style of winging. This style is excellent for giving the fly a streamlined shape when being retrieved through the water. The following sea trout flies are dressed with 'Delta' flytails and 'killer' style wings.

### The Keeper
*Tail*   Orange fly tail
*Body*   Yellow wool ribbed gold oval

*Wings*   Cock pheasant green rump – killer style
*Hackle*   Long fibre green rump
*Hook*   Longshank size 6 or 8.

I designed the original dressing of the Keeper in the early seventies. For many years it was one of the numerous patterns that I experimented with. In the early eighties I gave Dave Clark some dressings of this as yet unnamed fly to try. He and his guests did so well with this pattern fishing for sea trout that he came back for more. Dave is the head gamekeeper of a large sporting estate and is partly responsible for the success of the Keeper series flies. It was from the results of his testing and others that the Keeper series of flies evolved and the names I have given them. The original patterns were dressed with a feather slip from a goose feather for the tail.

### Headkeeper
*Tail*   Orange fly tail
*Body*   Peacock herl
*Wing*   Melanistic cock pheasant rump – killer style
*Cheeks*   Jungle cock or substitute

### Underkeeper
*Tail*   Orange fly tail
*Body*   Silver tinsel ribbed oval
*Wing*   Cock pheasant green rump – killer style
*Hackle*   Green rump
*Cheeks*   Jungle cock

For the Keeper and Underkeeper dyed red feather slips from a goose shoulder can be added on the side of the wing; this at times appears to make the flies more effective.

### Peacock Fly
*Tail*   Orange fly tail
*Body*   Silver tinsel ribbed oval
*Wing*   Peacock blue neck – killer style
*Hackle*   Blue peacock wound as collar

### Yellow Mallard
*Tail*   Yellow fly tail
*Body*   Yellow wool
*Wings*   Grey mallard flank – killer style
*Hackle*   Grey mallard dyed yellow

### Teal Lure
*Tail*   Green fly tail
*Body*   Yellow wool
*Wings*   Teal flank feathers – killer style
*Hackle*   Yellow cock

Killer style wings require whole feathers; each fly can have two or four feathers, it is the tyer's choice. The easy way to tie in whole feather wings is to strip the feather to the required size, tie in the feather by its stalk on the side of the hook with a couple of turns of silk, catch hold of the stalk and pull it towards the hookeye. When the leading fibres of the feather start going under the silk, stop – you will find this causes the feather to veil the body better as it makes for a more streamlined fly in the water. Tie in the hackle close to the hookeye, winding it as a collar and sweeping the fibres back over the wing and body and over tying. This helps to give a good streamlined shape to the lure while being fished.

### Black/Red

*Tail Body*   Black fly tail
*Thorax*   Bright red floss
*Hackle*   Dyed red cock
*Wing*   Black squirrel
*Hook*   Longshank size 6 or 8

Very effective sea trout pattern when used from late evening to dark. Even on dark nights it is surprising how well the fish see this fly and take it.

The plastic fly tails can be tied into virtually any fly pattern in place of the normal tail. There are also fly tails of special material that can be activated by light and will glow in the dark for a few minutes which are very useful for sea trout patterns when night fishing: activate the fly tail with torch light and then fish it.

When night fishing for sea trout it pays, unless you know the water you intend to fish, to make a thorough reconnaissance during the day. Study the water, check that there are fish running. Make a note of any bankside vegetation that may interfere with your backcast. During the day there may not appear to be any problems but in the dark the situation will change. That tall thistle, unnoticed in daylight, suddenly appears to pop up and catch your back cast in the dark, causing all sorts of problems. Select your fishing stand on the pool chosen and mark it ready for the evening's fishing, clearing any vegetation that is likely to interfere with your backcast. You should allow for the change of direction of your cast when you cover the fish that rises to the left or right. Take a note of the distance available for your casting and measure that distance off on your flyline to avoid catching the vegetation on the opposite bank in the dark. On big rivers this is not a problem, however most good sea trout fishing is found on small rivers or the tributaries of the large rivers.

For night fishing the normal practice is to arrive at the water in daylight and wait for it to get dark, at the same time familiarising oneself with the surroundings, making sure nothing has changed since the previous visit. As the light starts to fade the bats will appear, catching the insects which after a warm summer day are very plentiful. As soon as I see the bats I start fishing, usually commencing with a bright silver bodied fly; after a half hour or so it has not produced any results I will change to a darker pattern. In my experience the flies which have a slim streamlined shape in the water are usually the most effective; with fresh run sea trout the longer the fly the better is its killing power.

The streamer fly has always been very popular with North American fly fishers. The next series of dressings are American in origin; I do not know who their inventors are. These streamers have taken fish all over the world, including both Atlantic and Pacific salmon and they are very popular with trout and sea trout anglers.

### Black Ghost Streamer
*Tail*   Golden pheasant crest
*Body*   Black wool silver ribbing
*Hackle*   Golden pheasant crest or yellow hackle
*Wing*   Four white hackles
*Cheeks*   Jungle cock

### Grey Ghost Streamer
*Body*   Orange wool
*Hackle*   Strands of bronze peacock herl, then white bucktail, finally dyed yellow hackle
fibres
*Wing*   Four blue dun hackles
*Cheeks*   Lady Amherst pheasant tippets

### Brown Ghost Streamer
*Tag*   Silver tinsel
*Body*   Brown wool silver rib
*Hackle*   Strands of bronze peacock herl, then white bucktail, finally golden pheasant crest
*Wing*   Four red game hackles with golden pheasant topping over
*Shoulder*   Teal flank dyed brown
*Cheeks*   Jungle cock

### Royal Coachman Streamer
*Tail*   Golden pheasant tippets
*Body*   In three parts: peacock herl/red floss/peacock herl
*Wing*   Four white cock hackles
*Hackles*   Red game cock

### Parmachene Belle Streamer
*Tail*   Married red and yellow goose or duck
*Body*   Yellow wool ribbed gold oval
*Wing*   Two white cock hackles with two dyed red hackles outside
*Hackle*   Dyed red mixed with white cock hackles

### Chief Needabeh Streamer
*Tag*   Silver tinsel
*Body*   Scarlet floss ribbed oval silver
*Wing*   Two dyed yellow hackles with two orange outside
*Hackle*   Dyed yellow and scarlet cock
*Cheeks*   Jungle cock

These American streamers can be dressed on longshank hooks size 2, 4, 6, 8, using the larger sizes for salmon.

The next series of streamer flies are of my design. Thirty years ago there were not many UK-designed streamer fly patterns available and the UK fly-fisher was dependant on American designs. Pattern books of the early sixties could only give a few dressings designed by British fly-tyers. However with the influx of new British talent this situation has been long reversed and there are a wide selection of British streamer patterns available.

### Black Rock Streamer
*Body*   D.F.M. wool ribbed silver oval
*Wing*   Two black cock hackles with two grizzle outside
*Hackle*   Dyed red cock

*Plate 11* Spoons (*from the top*): Dexter Wedge, Black & Blue; Ogwen, Shaded Silver; Menal, Black & Yellow; Long Spoon, Black & Blue; Conway Spoon, Red & Black; Mepps Syclops, White; Ragot's Yann Spoon, Silver.
*Photo: Gordon Bellman*

*Plate 12* Plastic Tail Fly Lures *(first row, from the top)*: Black Lure, Yellow Cree Lure, Tadpole, Yellow Wiggler, Damsel Wiggler; *(second row, from the top)* Orange Lure, Green Badger Lure, White Wiggler, Bloodworm.
*Photo: Gordon Bellman*

This was my first ever streamer design, and on my first outing using it I took three brown trout within half hour of fishing.

## Black Streamer
*Tail*   Black cock hackle fibres
*Body*   Black wool ribbed gold oval
*Wing*   Four black hackles
*Hackle*   Black cock

Very good early season streamer; in cold conditions fish deep on sinking lines.

## Michael's Streamer
*Body*   Black wool ribbed wide silver tinsel
*Wing*   Four black cock hackles
*Hackle*   Dressed false – dyed yellow hackle fibres with dyed red hackle fibres
*Cheeks*   Jungle cock

This streamer can be fished deep or just under the surface. It will work just as well without the jungle cock cheeks, but I for one feel they make the fly more attractive to fish. The Michael's Streamer has for me lured more fish into my landing net than any other streamer, and the number of fish over three pounds in weight runs well into double figures.

## Orange Badger Streamer
*Tail*   Dyed red cock fibres
*Body*   Gold tinsel ribbed gold oval
*Wing*   Two badger hackles dyed hot orange
*Hackle*   Dyed red cock

Deadly streamer for rainbow trout, particularly if they are cruising in shoals on a regular beat. It is quite easy to have catches well into double figures, taking one or two fish out of the shoal every time its passes on its beat. Depending a little on how large an area the beat covers, it may be a case of a fish every few minutes or a fish every so often.

## Yellow Barred Rock Streamer
*Tail*   Brown hackle fibres
*Body*   Gold tinsel ribbed gold oval
*Wing*   Two grizzle hackles dyed yellow
*Hackle*   Red game dressed as collar

Useful streamer for both rainbow and brown trout. Very good in the shallows where the small bait fish are taking cover when the bigger trout are making their raids from deeper water. For catching the fry raiders use the lure on a floating line and retrieve in long uniform pulls, with short pauses in between.

## Ron Streamer
*Tail*   Dyed yellow hackle fibres
*Body*   D.F.M. scarlet wool ribbed silver oval
*Wing*   Four black cock hackles
*Hackle*   Dyed yellow cock

Most effective for rainbows and browns. Can be fished either with sinking or floating lines. More useful for browns when used with the sinking line. The rainbows will take also take it well on the bottom, but will take it rather better while it is being fished just under the surface on a floating line.

**Golden Cree Streamer**
*Body*   Gold tinsel ribbed gold oval
*Wing*   Four cree hackles dyed yellow
*Hackle*   Yellow cree cock

This dressing is very useful when the fry are in the margins; cast it out and strip back in long measured pulls. When large hatches of caenis occur just before sunset and the trout become pre-occupied with the broadwings, this streamer stripped across their noses will sometimes provoke a response.

# 11

# More Fly Lures

## Dan Bailey's Fly Shop (USA)

Dan Bailey moved to Livingston, Montana in 1938 and started building up his fly-tying business. After two years in Montana, his quality dry flies had gained quite a reputation in an area where dry fly-fishing was virtually unknown. As with any quality product, their fame was soon spread by the bush telegraph. This was the start of his mail order business with orders coming in from all over the USA. Dan Bailey's Fly Shop has its own fly-tying department in modern premises with good lighting, comfortable seating and fly bench layout for the tyers. This enables them to have full control over the quality, production and service which has ensured their domestic market has not been lost to the influx of third world flies.

The company is now under the direction of Dan Bailey's son, John, who had watched the business develop as he grew up, hearing all the fishing tales and which fly patterns were most effective. Today many of these flies are virtually unknown, lost in the mist of time. As time moved on new materials became available which made for new patterns and improvements on old patterns. The new and unusual materials being incorporated into fly dressing made it necessary for new fly-tying techniques to be developed in some cases.

John Bailey is not content to rely on the proven patterns of the past, he spends hours testing and developing new materials for his flies. Many of the best ideas come from his customers, which he follows up. Before any new patterns are released they have come through a comprehensive stream testing and assessment by John and his staff.

### John Bailey's Lures

**Brown Woolly Bugger**
*Tail*   Black marabou fibres
*Body*   Brown chenille
*Hackle*   Brown cock, palmer wound

**Olive Woolly Bugger**
*Tail*   Black marabou fibres
*Body*   Olive chenille
*Hackle*   Olive cock, palmer wound

**Black Woolly Bugger**
*Tail*   Black marabou fibres
*Body*   Black chenille
*Hackle*   Black cock, palmer wound

Hooks, longshank sizes 4, 6, 8, 10.

This fly is a great favourite for big brown trout on the lakes. It is renowned for its ability to attract trout in small streams when they are feeding selectively. The marabou tail together with soft palmered hackle gives the Woolly Bugger a very enticing action.

### Black Flash-A-Bugger
*Tail*   Black marabou and silver Flashabou mixed
*Body*   Black chenille ribbed silver tinsel
*Hackle*   Palmered black cock

### Olive Flash-A-Bugger
*Tail*   Black marabou and silver Flashabou mixed
*Body*   Olive chenille ribbed silver tinsel
*Hackle*   Palmered black cock

### Brown Flash-A-Bugger
*Tail*   Black marabou and silver Flashabou mixed
*Body*   Brown chenille ribbed silver tinsel
*Hackle*   Palmered black cock

### Red Head Flash-A-Bugger
*Tail*   Black marabou and silver Flashabou mixed
*Body*   Black chenille ribbed silver tinsel
*Hackle*   Palmered black cock
*Head*   Red chenille muddler type

Hooks, longshank sizes 4, 6, 8, 10.

Big heavily-weighted Flash-A-Buggers have taken large numbers of browns, rainbows and steelhead. When fished deep they have always taken their share of big fish. The Red Head Flash-A-Bugger is especially effective for spawn feeding fish which have been following the salmon.

### Brown Crayfish
*Tail*   Deer hair spun and clipped, flanked grey squirrel tail hair
*Body*   Brown chenille
*Head*   Deer hair spun and clipped

### Olive Crayfish
*Tail*   Deer hair spun and clipped, flanked grey squirrel tail hair
*Body*   Olive chenille
*Head*   Deer hair spun and clipped

To dress the crayfish, first spin the deer hair on the end of the hook and trim, thus leaving a small deer hair ball. Take a reasonably sized bunch of hair from a grey squirrel tail. Split into two bunches and tie each bunch alongside the hookshank with the hair pointing out past the deer hair ball forming the vee tail. Tie in chenille and wind, finish off with a muddler type deer hair head. The most suitable hook sizes are longshank 4, 6, 8. In waters where they occur, cray-fish are an important part of the trout's diet. John Bailey's pattern is particularly effective for the various species of trout and bass.

### Light Spruce Streamer
*Tail*   Peacock sword feather
*Body*   Reds floss, peacock herl
*Wing*   Badger cock hackles
*Hackle*   Badger wound as collar

**Dark Spruce Streamer**
*Tail*  Peacock sword feather
*Body*  Red floss, peacock herl
*Wing*  Cree cock hackles
*Hackle*  Cree wound as collar

The original Light Spruce fly was a popular wet fly pattern in the Northwest of the USA. Dan Bailey adapted it to a streamer style, and it soon became one of his favourites for large trout. The long hacklewing dressed in streamer mode improved the action of the pattern and gave it a very enticing lifelike movement in the water. Because of the success of the Light Spruce, the Dark Spruce was developed and also proved to be an equally effective fish catcher.

**Black Electric Sculpin**
*Tail*  Black marabou mixed lure flash tinsel
*Body*  Black crystal chenille
*Hackle*  Black cock
*Head*  Black chenille

**Brown Electric Sculpin**
*Tail*  Brown marabou mixed lure flash tinsel
*Body*  Brown crystal chenille
*Hackle*  Brown cock
*Head*  Brown chenille

Hook sizes, longshank 2, 4, 6.

The muddler-shaped heads on the Electric Sculpin help them to sink better than sculpins dressed with deer hair heads, and the crystal chenille gives the lures added sparkle in the water. For the hackle use the lower fluffy part of the feather; this will give a marabou effect to the dressing.

**Black Woolly Worm**
*Body*  Black chenille
*Hackle*  Palmered grizzle cock
*Tail*  Dyed red goat hair

**Black and Brown Woolly**
*Body*  Black chenille
*Hackle*  Palmered furnace cock
*Tail*  Dyed red goat hair

**Yellow Woolly Worm**
*Body*  Yellow chenille
*Hackle*  Palmered grizzle cock
*Tail*  Dyed red goat hair

The woollies are designed for bottom fishing and should be dressed on longshank hooks and weighted.

**Brown Bomber**
*Tail*  Dyed red feather fibre
*Body*  Black chenille
*Hackle*  Furnace cock

The Brown Bomber is similar to the Woolly worm, but instead of a palmered hackle down the body, its body consist of three segments, each one butted with a furnace hackle, giving the body three distinct bands.

**Black Leach**
*Tail*   Black cock fibres
*Body*   Black wool
*Wing*   Black cock hackles
*Head*   Black Ostrich herl

Lightweight pattern, do not overdress; keep the wool body slim. When being fished in the water it must look just like a pencil lead.

**Rusty Squirrel Optic**
*Tail*   Black squirrel hair
*Body*   Goldfingering floss
*Wing*   Grey squirrel
*Head*   Orange deer hair spun and clipped
*Eyes*   Two gold beads

Useful pattern for salmon and trout in Alaska. The bead eyes help to make it sink quickly.

**White Wiggle Tail**
*Tail*   White marabou
*Body*   Pink wool ribbed silver tinsel
*Hackle*   Flashabou silver tinsel

Popular in Alaska, used mainly for salmon. Equally effective for rainbows, Dolly Varden, grayling and browns.

**Orange Comet**
*Tail*   Brown bucktail
*Body*   Stripped peacock eye
*Hackle*   Orange cock, half palmered
*Head*   Red silk

Dress the bucktail long – it must be a little longer than the fly. The hackle is wound halfway down the shank palmer style. Finish off the head with red silk, bright and bold. Useful steelhead pattern, equally good for all fish species found in northern waters.

**Fall Favourite**
*Body*   Silver tinsel
*Hackle*   Dyed red cock
*Wing*   Amber bucktail

**Orange Demon**
*Tail*   Orange and yellow fibres
*Body*   Yellow chenille
*Hackle*   Orange cock
*Wing*   Black bucktail

**Polar Shrimp**
*Tail*   Dyed red cock fibres
*Body*   Orange chenille ribbed silver tinsel

*Hackle*   Hot orange cock
*Wing*   White bucktail

### Skunk
*Tail*   Dyed red cock fibres
*Body*   Black chenille ribbed silver tinsel
*Hackle*   Black cock
*Wing*   White marabou

These four patterns are good allrounders and will take all species of game fish in virtually all types of waters.

### Black Bastard
*Tail*   Black squirrel tail hair, dressed long
*Body*   Yellow chenille, in three parts each part butted with black hackle

This pattern was originated by Doug Robertson for steelhead on the Sustut river, and it has been the top fly there for many years. Its enticing, pulsating action also makes it equally attractive to many other species.

Dan Bailey uses Mylar tubing for the bodies of the next three lures. This material makes a very realistic-looking fish scale body. Dressing the bucktail over and under the hook suggest the different minnow body colours and imparts 'life' to the streamers in the whole effect while being fished.

### Mickey Finn Mylar
*Silk*   Red
*Body*   Silver Mylar tubing
*Hackle*   Yellow bucktail
*Wing*   Red bucktail with yellow bucktail over

### Silver Doctor Mylar
*Silk*   Red
*Body*   Silver Mylar tubing
*Hackle*   White bucktail
*Wing*   Blue-red-yellow bucktail, peacock herl over

### Integration Mylar
*Silk*   Red
*Body*   Silver Mylar tubing
*Hackle*   White bucktail
*Wing*   Black bucktail mixed crystal hair

Hook sizes longshank 2, 4, 6, 8, 10.

When tying in the Mylar tube at the tail end, make a wide bold whipping of red silk and varnish. This gives a bright red tag to the lure which makes a good aiming point for any predator. All three dressings can have crystal hair mixed into the bucktail wings and hackles which will give the streamers added sparkle in the water. The heads can be just varnished, or varnished and then white eyes with black centres painted on.

The Electric Buggers are dressed with long fibre chenille with tinsel mixed with the fibres. Ordinary chenilles do not have enough motion when in the water to make these patterns work as they should.

### Black Electric Bugger
*Tail*　Black marabou mixed peacock sword
*Body*　Black flash chenille
*Body Hackle*　Black cock palmered
*Hackle*　Black cock

### White Electric Bugger
*Tail*　Black marabou
*Body*　White flash chenille
*Body Hackle*　Black cock palmered
*Hackle*　Black cock

### Red Electric Bugger
*Tail*　Black marabou mixed grizzle cock fibres
*Body*　Red flash chenille
*Body Hackle*　Black cock palmered
*Hackle*　Black cock

Hook sizes longshank 2, 4, 6, 8. Useful patterns for all species of trout, can be fished deep or sub-surface.

### Black Nosed Dace
*Body*　Silver tinsel
*Wing*　White bucktail with black tail hair over

### Little Brown Trout
*Tail*　Golden pheasant tippet
*Body*　 White wool ribbed silver oval
*Wing*　Grey squirrel tail

### Little Brook Trout
*Tail*　Green cock fibres
*Tag*　Bright red floss
*Body*　White wool ribbed silver oval
*Hackle*　Hot orange tail hair dressed short
*Wing*　Red-white-green bucktail, grey squirrel over

### Little Rainbow Trout
*Tail*　Green cock fibres
*Body*　White wool ribbed silver tinsel
*Hackle*　White calftail dressed short
*Wing*　White-green bucktail, grey squirrel over

Hook sizes longshank 2, 4, 6, 8, 10. Useful fry-imitating patterns for the young of the various species. Effective most of the time when the fry are about, will take fish throughout the season.

### Skykomish Sunrise
*Tail*　Red and yellow bucktail mixed
*Body*　Orange chenille ribbed silver tinsel

*Hackle*   Red and white cock wound together as collar
*Hook*   Longshank sizes 2, 4, 6, 8

A useful and most popular steelhead pattern. It should also be equally as effective for its counterpart – the sea trout.

## Babine Special
*Body*   Two parts, orange chenille butted red and white hackles, then orange chenille again
*Hackle*   White cock
*Silk*   Red
*Hook*   Wide gape 2, 4, 6, 8

Dyed orange deer hair spun and clipped can be used instead of chenille. This brightly coloured pattern is supposed to represent salmon eggs and is used in Alaskan waters to take salmon, steelhead and rainbow trout. There is no reason why this dressing should not be equally effective for all types of waters and species.

   To dress the Babine Special so that it looks like a pair of salmon eggs stuck together, first tie the orange chenille at the hook bend and wind half-way up the hookshank, forming it into a muddler type ball. Now secure and cut off any surplus chenille. Tie in red and white cock hackles and wind as a collar. Secure the hackles and tie in orange chenille and form the second muddler type ball. Now complete with a white hackle and whip finish.

## Rabbit Matuka White
*Body*   Pearl
*Hackle*   Dyed red cock
*Wing*   Strip of white rabbit fur

## Rabbit Matuka Olive
*Body*   Pearl
*Hackle*   Dyed red cock
*Wing*   Strip of dyed olive rabbit fur

## Rabbit Matuka Black
*Body*   Pearl
*Hackle*   Dyed red cock
*Wing*   Strip of black rabbit fur

The wing of the Rabbit Matuka is a narrow strip of rabbit fur on the skin which is tied on top of the hookshank to form the wing.

## Olive Matuka
*Body*   Olive floss ribbed silver tinsel
*Wing*   Blackcock hackles
*Hackle*   Olive cock

## Black Matuka
*Body*   Black floss ribbed silver tinsel
*Wing*   Black cock
*Hackle*   Black cock

## Brown Matuka
*Body*   Brown floss ribbed silver tinsel
*Wing*   Brown cree
*Hackle*   Brown cock

The Matuka is a New Zealand style of dressing for their streamers. The winging material is prepared and then lashed down along the length of the body; this design keeps the feathers from wrapping around the hook when in use.

Rabbit fur dressed in Matuka style does not, if properly tied, twist around the hook shank. When in use it creates a lifelike pulsating movement rather like a breathing action.

The Muddler was created by Dan Gapen to imitate the bait fish of North America. This he did rather well – perhaps never before has a single fly produced such outstanding results. Dan Bailey refined and popularized the standard dressing from the Catskills to the Rockies.

Probably the Muddler Minnow is the nearest we are likely to get to a 'magic' fly. This mixture of fur, feather and hair has been used to imitate small fish, aquatic creatures and creatures which fall on the waters from time to time.

### Muddler Minnow
*Tail*	Oak turkey
*Body*	Gold tinsel ribbed gold wire
*Wing*	Grey squirrel flanked by oak turkey strips
*Head*	Natural deer hair spun and clipped

### White Muddler
*Tail*	White goose
*Butt*	Red ostrich
*Body*	White wool
*Wing*	White calf tail flanked by white goose
*Head*	One spinning of natural deer hair then white

### Yellow Muddler
*Tail*	Yellow goose
*Body*	Yellow wool
*Wing*	Grey squirrel flanked by yellow goose
*Head*	Natural deer hair spun and clipped

Hook size longshank 2, 4, 6, 8, 10

Another useful pattern is the Spuddler and it is considered to imitate the sculpin more closely than the standard Muddler. The Spuddler is a combination of the Muddler and the Spruce Fly Streamer and has taken many large trout in a wide variety of waters.

### Spuddler
*Tail*	Brown squirrel tail hair
*Body*	White cream wool
*Wing*	Dark Cree hackles
*Thorax*	Red wool
*Head*	Deerhair spun and clipped
*Hook*	Longshank size 2, 4, 6, 8

The weighted Spuddler fished deep is very effective for taking big trout when conditions for normal fishing are poor.

Muddler Minnows were first introduced into the UK in 1967, the Spuddler following in 1971. Since that time a whole host of variations on the basic designs have made their presence felt. All these mutants have one thing in common with the original dressing: spun and clipped deer hair head. There is no doubt that many of the variations are extremely effective, but whether or not they surpass the originals I do not know, only time will tell.

It was in 1985, I think, when Chris Martindale of Lancashire devised the next three dressings. He designed them especially for the wilder waters, where the truly wild brown trout live. They are also very effective for both brown and rainbow trout in many of the water supply reservoirs.

**Green A**
*Tail*  Fibres from cock pheasant tail
*Body*  Two parts, D.F.M. lime green wool then peacock herl
*Wing*  Cock pheasant tail fibres encircling hookshank

**Blue Neck**
*Tail*  Teal flank fibres
*Body*  Two parts, silver tinsel then royal blue wool
*Wing*  Cock pheasant tail fibres encircling hookshank

**Yellow Belle**
*Tail*  Golden pheasant yellow rump fibres
*Body*  Two parts, gold tinsel then yellow wool
*Wing*  Cock pheasant tail fibres encircling hookshank
*Hackle*  Yellow squirrel tail hair dressed short

Dress Martindale's flies in the normal manner except for the pheasant fibre wing. This must be spread equally around the hookshank to produce an even uniform wing. The length of the wing should be halfway down the tail fibres. When being fished, this design with its streamline shape will look like a small fish darting through the water. It is very important that the cock pheasant tail wing is sparsely dressed, thus showing the body colours through the wing fibres when wet. Hook is longshank size 6, 8, 10.

Peter Williams, a professional fly-tyer from Carmarthen, Wales, sent me the following three dressings which he indicated were effective for sea trout, salmon and trout. They can be dressed on any hook-size but he personally preferred the smaller sizes. He did not give any names for these patterns.

**Peter's Mallard Special**
*Body*  Black seal's fur ribbed broad silver tinsel
*Wing*  Bronze mallard shoulder

This fly, dressed on a size six hook, made it possible for Peter Williams to take two grilse and seven sea trout in an evening's fishing.

**Peter's Red Cree Special**
*Body*  Red D.F.M. floss ribbed silver tinsel
*Hackle*  Cree cock swept back to veil body

**Peter's Golden Cree Special**
*Tail*  Golden pheasant tail fibres
*Body*  Golden pheasant tail fibres ribbed gold tinsel

*Hackle*   Cree cock
*Cheeks*   Jungle cock

Dress the cree patterns with long fibred hackles using hackles larger than the ones you would normally use for the hook size being dressed. This will allow the fibres to extend well beyond the hookshank, thus giving an attractive shape to the fly while being retrieved. The tail for the Golden Cree should be dressed long.

An old pattern which I found to be extremely effective, but appears to have been forgotten in recent times, is the 'Missionary'. This pattern was developed by Captain J.J. Dunn for use on Blagdon lake in the early part of the century. It proved to be deadly and its reputation spread worldwide; so much so that there were many letters to the angling press from fly-fishers who had taken exceptional bags of trout with it.

A variation of the Missionary was developed in due course and this was dressed with an orange hackle instead of the white hackle. This dressing proved to be just as effective as the original in taking fish over a wide variety of waters. It was proving particularly effective in New Zealand in the 1920s.

**Missionary**
*Tail*   White cock fibres
*Body*   White wool ribbed silver tinsel
*Wing*   Black cock hackles flanked strips of teal
*Hackle*   White cock

**Orange Missionary**
*Tail*   Orange cock fibres
*Body*   White wool ribbed silver tinsel
*Wing*   Black cock hackles flanked strips of teal
*Hackle*   Orange cock

Hooks for both varieties: longshank size 6, 8, 10.

Many of the water supply reservoirs in Britain have populations of coarse fish. Where they occur, the fry of these coarse fish have become part of the normal diet for the rainbow and brown because they are there to be taken. In most waters perch fry have always figured highly in the diet of the larger trout either in the natural lakes or reservoirs. In reservoirs, roach, rudd and many other coarse fish have become established, so much so in some cases they have become a nuisance and only regular netting and trapping has kept their numbers down.

The next three dressings are intended to represent the fry of the perch, roach and rudd.

**Perch Fry** (Lewis)
*Tail*   Two cree cock hackles trimmed to fishtail shape
*Body*   Cream wool ribbed brown floss
*Hackle*   Dyed olive and red hackles mixed
*Wing*   Four cree cock hackles

**Roach Fry** (Train)
*Tail*   Grey mallard flank fibres
*Body*   White wool ribbed silver tinsel
*Hackle*   White hen

*Wing*   Blue – white bucktail with black squirrel over
*Cheek*   Jungle cock

**Rudd Fry** (Unknown)
*Tail*   Olive cock fibres
*Body*   Bronze Goldfingering floss
*Hackle*   Claret
*Wing*   White calf tail with grey squirrel over

*Hook size*: longshank 6 or 8

Ragot of Loudeac produce the following lures for the trout in the stillwaters of Europe.

**Marabou Yellow**
*Tail*   Dyed red cock fibres
*Body*   Silver tinsel
*Hackle*   Dyed red cock
*Wing*   Yellow marabou with peacock sword over

**Marabou White**
*Tail*   Dyed red cock fibres
*Body*   Silver tinsel
*Hackle*   Dyed red cock
*Wing*   White marabou with peacock sword over

**Marabou Black**
*Tail*   Dyed red cock fibres
*Body*   Silver tinsel
*Hackle*   Dyed red cock
*Wing*   Black marabou with peacock sword over

*Hook size*: longshank 6 or 8. They can be fished using the same techniques as any other lures and are very good for taking fish as they sink after making a cast.

The next series of lures are produced by H. Turrall & Co., Dolton, Devon, England. This fly-tying company was started many years ago by Colonel Hugh Turrall, a keen fly-fisherman who was very much influenced by the fly-dressing of R.S. Austin, a famous fly-tyer in Devon in 1890. Turrall organised the local fly-tyers and developed a cottage industry producing flies for use in the waters of the West Country. During the next forty years up to the time of writing, Turrall's have established themselves in the international market and supply fishing flies worldwide. Under the direction of Tod Marshman, Turralls produce a wide selection of fly types for all waters and applications. The following flies are my selection of some of their streamers and lures.

**Cat Whiskers**
*Body*   Yellow chenille
*Wing*   White marabou

**Christmas Tree**
*Tail*   Yellow floss
*Body*   Black chenille ribbed oval tinsel
*Hackle*   Orange floss
*Wing*   Black marabou

**Hornberg**
*Body*   Yellow wool
*Wing*   Grey mallard flank – killer style
*Hackle*   Grizzle wound as collar

**Viva**
*Tail*   Green wool
*Body*   Black chenille ribbed silver oval
*Wing*   Black squirrel

**Jack Frost**
*Tail*   Orange floss
*Body*   White wool
*Hackle*   Orange and white hackles wound together
*Wing*   White marabou

**Undertaker**
*Tail*   White and black cock fibres
*Body*   White chenille
*Hackle*   Black cock fibres dressed false
*Wing*   White cock hackles with black hackles outside

**Doc Spratley** (Canada)
*Tail*   Guinea fowl hackle fibres
*Body*   Black chenille ribbed silver oval
*Hackle*   Guinea fowl
*Wing*   Pheasant tail fibres or brown cock

**Thingeyingur** (Iceland)
*Body*   Dark green floss ribbed oval tinsel
*Hackle*   Dark brown bucktail
*Wing*   Dyed yellow bucktail

**Supervisor Tandem** (USA)
*Rear Hook*   Orange wool tag, silver body
*Front Hook*   Silver tinsel
*Wing*   Marabou dyed lemon yellow.

All the above patterns are dressed on longshank hooks, apart from the Supervisor, and all are generally effective for game fish in most parts of the world. The Cat Whiskers, Christmas Tree, Jack Frost, Hornberg, Undertaker, and Viva are good throughout the season in British reservoirs, particularly when used with sinking lines in cold weather for rainbow trout.

The next three dressings were produced in the sixties by the world renowned company of C. Farlow & Co. Ltd, Pall Mall, London. These streamers in their day took their share of fish, but in recent years have appeared to have fallen out of favour. However I think they are too good to be lost and I have included them for you.

**Silver Murderers**
*Tail*   Lime fluorescent wool
*Body*   Embossed silver tinsel

*Wings*   Two grizzle cock hackles
*Cheeks*   Jungle cock
*Hackle*   Yellow cock wound as collar

## Black Murderers
*Tail*   Red fluorescent wool
*Body*   Black floss ribbed white fluorescent silk
*Wings*   Two black cock hackles
*Cheeks*   Jungle cock
*Hackle*   Red cock wound as collar

## Gold Murderers
*Tail*   Red fluorescent wool
*Body*   Gold embossed tinsel
*Wings*   Two grizzle hackles
*Cheeks*   Jungle cock
*Hackle*   Red cock wound as collar

*Hook sizes*: longshank 4, 6, 8. The heads should be finished in black.

# 12

# Leadheads, Poppers and Others

Wake flies and poppers are surface lures that are fished so as to cause a disturbance on the water like a wounded or crippled minnow, which will bring up the hungry predator to slash at the lure. For floating lures I use buoyant material such as deer hair, cork or balsa wood. A method of fishing I find successful when the lake trout are coming into the shallows chasing fry is to allow the lure to float with the natural water movement and then give it a twitch or two. Other creatures can be imitated and fished on the surface, such as frogs, grasshoppers, stoneflies and crickets and I have devised the following to imitate them. How you fish these floating lures is important and careful observation of the action of naturals when on the water will help you to develop a technique for imparting a realistic movement to the lure. I like to give the line a short jerk thus causing the lure to go under the water and pop up again; this can be quite effective at times, bringing fish from some distance away. Often the first thing you become aware of is a bow wave heading for your lure at speed; it is quite a problem to choose between moving the lure or leaving it floating still; very exciting fishing can be had using these tactics.

**Minnow Surface Lure**
*Tail*   Grey white bucktail clipped fishtail shape
*Body*   Cork slips whipped on hookshank, white raffia wound to fish body shape, ribbed with wide silver tinsel and varnished
*Head*   Deer hair – first spinning dyed red hair followed by spinnings of natural colour deer hair
*Hook*   Longshank 6, or 8

To tie the floating minnow, wind the silk down the hookshank, leaving the first part clear for spinning the deer hair. Tie in the bucktail for the tail the length of the silk-covered hookshank and clip the loose end of the bucktail to a fish-like shape. Now tie in the cork slips which have been shaped rather like a fish body on each side of the shank; overtie the cork with plenty of turns with the silk to make the body really secure. Tie in raffia and silver tinsel, wind the raffia into a streamlined fish shape and rib with silver tinsel and then varnish liberally. When the varnish is dry, first spin in a pinch of dyed red deer hair to simulate the red of gills, then complete the head with light coloured natural hair and clip the hair to match the taper of the body with a torpedo point to the head; leave some of the longer hair at the side just in front of the body to simulate fins.

**Grasshopper Lure**
*Body*   Yellow green dyed deer hair
*Wing*   Brown bucktail trimmed square with rear of body
*Hackle*   Grizzle cock dyed green and clipped

Dress the deer hair body in the normal manner and clip it to a grasshopper shape. For tying in the bucktail wing it is important that you build the silk bed foundation up level with the deer hair body so that the bucktail lies level. If you leave any sort of step down from the deer hair body, it will flare up as you pull your first turn of silk tight while tying in the bucktail and you will have the individual hairs pointing in all directions. Make sure the foundation is as high or slightly higher than the body, tie in the bucktail with three loose turns of silk and gently pull tight. If all is well, complete the tying-in of the wing in the normal manner. After tying and winding the grizzle hackle, clip it within 1·25 cm ($^1/_2$ in) of the hookshank. The hooksize can be longshank size 6 to 10 — anything smaller would be the same as a normal sedge. I consider the best size to be a light wire longshank size 6.

### Frog Surface Lure
*Legs*   Natural bucktail twisted, secure at the end with fuse wire
*Body*   Spun deer hair trimmed to shape

Use a size 2 or 4 lightwire longshank hook. Wind on a few turns of silk at the hook bend. Lay your bucktail on the hookshank so that the turns of silk are about halfway up its length; split the bucktail each side of the silk into two bunches; double the forward two bunches back over on top of the rear two bunches; overtie and separate with turns of silk. Twist the two bunches of bucktail and secure the loose ends with fuse wire, leaving enough hair to form the frog's feet. When the rear legs are complete, varnish the wire whippings and turns of silk on the hookshank. Now spin the deer hair body and clip to shape. Complete the front legs by the same method and colour the body with a felt pen.

### Stone Hopper Lure
*Tail*   Dyed red bucktail clipped square
*Body*   Slips of cork, overtied with yellow silk
*Wing*   Grey squirrel tail flanked by mottled turkey
*Head*   Natural deer hair clipped

My Stone Hopper dressing is a useful general attractor pattern — very effective fished in a fast streamy run. Both the Stone Hopper and the Frog Lure are useful for pike and large trout.

### Brown Wake Fly
*Tail*   Dyed red bucktail clipped square
*Wing*   Grey squirrel tail flanked by brown turkey
*Head*   Dyed brown deer hair partly clipped

### White Wake Fly
*Tail*   Dyed red bucktail clipped square
*Wing*   White bucktail flanked by grey turkey
*Head*   White deer hair partly clipped

Dress the wake flies on longshank size 6 hooks. Tie the bucktail hair tail so that it encircles the hookshank, making it possible to overtie with tight turns of silk, thus making a lightweight body. Clip the tail square about 2·5 cm (1 in) long. Leave the deer hair head quite bushy, trimming it so that it tapers down towards the hookeye. Fish the Wake Fly with long slow pulls so that it leaves a wake across the surface of the water. When the fish chases it you will see a big bow wave coming up behind the lure.

The following floating lures are produced by Don Bailey's Fly Shop for a wide variety of waters.

### John's Elk Hair Hopper
*Tail*   Dyed red Bucktail
*Body*   Polypropylene yarn, brown palmer hackle
*Wing*   Bucktail
*Hackle*   Brown cock
*Hook*   Wide gape size 4, 6, 8, 10

### Elk Hair Salmon Fly
*Tail*   Bucktail
*Body*   Orange polypropylene, brown palmer hackle
*Wing*   Bucktail
*Hackle*   Furnace cock
*Hook*   Longshank 4, 6, 8

### Sofa Pillow
*Tail*   Dyed red feather fibre
*Body*   Red polypropylene
*Wing*   Bucktail
*Hackle*   Light ginger cock
*Hook*   Longshank 4, 6, 8

### Bullet Salmon Fly
*Body*   Black bucktail ribbed orange floss
*Wing*   Black bucktail
*Head*   Loose ends of bucktail wing doubled back and overtied

### Yellowstone Hopper
*Tail*   Bucktail
*Body*   Deer hair clipped
*Wing*   Bucktail
*Head*   Loose ends of bucktail wing doubled back and overtied

The Yellowstone River in America has a prolific salmon fly hatch which generally occurs early in July. Flies can measure up to 6·5 cm (2½ in) long. When this occurs the patterns given are, as a rule, the most effective. There is no reason why they should not work just as well dapping for salmon and sea trout in the Scottish lochs and as wake flies on many other waters.

The next selection of flies from Don Bailey's Fly Shop are deer hair bass bugs designed by H.G. Tapply. These bugs are dressed completely with deer hair, usually in two colours and are extremely light, high floating and durable. Cast one of these bugs in clear water between the weed banks, let it lie for a while then impart some life to it by moving the rod tip. The movement and burbling noise made by the flat deer hair front end will sometimes receive immediate attention from the fish. Construction of these bugs is a long bucktail tail, then tapered deer hair bodies with a flat front looking forward.

**Halloween**
*Tail*   Black bucktail
*Body*   Rear black deer hair, then red deer hair clipped

**Red Head**
*Tail*   White bucktail
*Body*   Rear white deer hair, then red deer hair clipped.

**Blonde**
*Tail*   White bucktail
*Body*   Rear white deer hair, then yellow deer hair clipped

**Grey Popper**
*Tail*   Two grizzle hackles
*Body*   Grizzle hackle then natural deer hair clipped

To dress these poppers, first tie two grizzle hackles to form the tail. The hackles should be a little longer than the hook. Part the hackles with turns of silk to form a vee and tie in the body hackle close to the hook head and wind. Now spin the deer hair on the remainder of the bare hookshank and clip. The body should be bell-shaped with a flat front. These poppers are intended primarily for large and small-mouth bass but they will work well for other species particularly if the water and conditions are suitable. Effective for rainbow trout and pike if popped on the edge of weed banks.

## The Leadhead Lure

**Black Leadhead**
*Body*   Black wool
*Wing*   Marabou black fibres mixed silver Flashabou
*Head*   Lead shot or metal bead

**Yellow Leadhead**
*Body*   Yellow wool
*Wing*   Yellow marabou fibres mixed gold Flashabou
*Head*   Lead shot or metal bead

**Orange Leadhead**
*Body*   Orange wool
*Wing*   Orange marabou fibres mixed red Flashabou
*Head*   Lead shot or metal bead

Tie the marabou fibres with the Flashabou mixed together just behind the metal head so that it encircles the hookshank like a collar. Another technique for weighting the lure is lead or copper wire. After completing the fly, leave enough room on the hookshank just behind the eye to allow a ball of lead or copper wire to be formed. This method will allow double and treble hooks to be dressed with a metal head quite easily.

My original series of Flasher flies are dressed on longshank treble hooks for salmon. I have since dressed them on longshank and double hooks with lead wire heads and they have proved to be successful for trout and sea trout, river or lake fishing. The following patterns can be dressed on virtually any hook, single, double or treble, providing the hookshank is of reasonable length to be able to take the dressing plus the lead head.

**April Flasher**
*Tail*    Lureflash red crystal hair
*Body*    Black wool ribbed silver oval
*Wing*    Orange calf tail mixed red crystal hair
*Head*    Lead or copper wire

**Black Flasher**
*Tail*    Lureflash green crystal hair
*Body*    Black wool ribbed silver oval
*Wing*    Black squirrel mixed silver crystal hair
*Head*    Lead or copper wire

**Blue Flasher**
*Tail*    Lureflash blue crystal hair
*Body*    Silver tinsel ribbed oval
*Wing*    White calf tail mixed blue crystal hair
*Head*    Lead or copper wire

**Claret Flasher**
*Tail*    Claret cock fibres mixed red crystal hair
*Body*    Copper tinsel ribbed copper wire
*Wing*    Claret calf tail mixed red Flashabou
*Head*    Lead or copper wire

**Golden Flasher**
*Tail*    Lureflash yellow crystal hair
*Body*    Gold tinsel, ribbed gold oval
*Wing*    Brown calf tail mixed gold Flashabou
*Hackle*    Long fibre-dyed lemon yellow cock
*Head*    Lead or copper wire

**June Flasher**
*Tail*    Lureflash green crystal hair
*Body*    Peacock herl, ribbed yellow floss
*Wing*    Yellow-brown calf tail mixed red and blue Flashabou
*Head*    Lead or copper wire

**Magenta Flasher**
*Tail*    Magenta wool
*Body*    Black wool, ribbed silver tinsel
*Wing*    Black marabou mixed red and silver Flashabou
*Head*    Lead or copper wire

**Red Flasher**
*Tail*    Red Flashabou
*Body*    Gold tinsel, ribbed red floss
*Wing*    Brown calf tail mixed red crystal hair
*Head*    Lead or copper wire

**Orange Flasher**
*Tail*  Orange crystal hair
*Body*  Gold tinsel, ribbed oval
*Wing*  Orange marabou mixed gold Flashabou
*Head*  Lead or copper wire

**White Flasher**
*Tail*  Lureflash twinkle luminous pink
*Body*  White wool, ribbed silver oval
*Wing*  White marabou mixed red Flashabou
*Head*  Lead or copper wire

The Flasher fly wings should be dressed so that they encircle the hookshank; the wire heads can be varnished various colours. I always varnish my heads red as this seems to offer an aiming point for the taking fish.

To fish the lead head, after casting it out allow it to sink; most of the takes will come at this point. The weighted front of the lure causes it to dive head first and the fluttering of the winging and tail material with its erratic sinking action makes it attractive and the fish will really hit the lure. These lures are tricky to cast on light tackle as the weight of the lure makes smooth casting difficult; you will have to slow your action and line speed down.

**Tubes**
The tube fly came into being around the mid-fifties. This design consists of the fly being dressed on the tube and fished with a treble hook on the end of the line. Most manufactured tubes have a cavity in the tube to take the head of the treble hook thus ensuring the hook is always in perfect alignment. When the fish takes, the tube will slide up the line out of the way.

The initial tube fly designs were intended for salmon fishing but the tube fly can be used for all species of fish, freshwater or saltwater. The tubing can be of any material from plastic to metal. They can be cast or trolled and made to any size. Long brass tubes are very effective trolling lures for big lake trout particularly if you put a small flicker spinning blade on the line in front of the tube.

The plastic tube fly, because of its light construction, makes it an excellent design for river fishing for salmon. Probably the most widely used method of fishing the tube fly is to cast it out on the fly rod slightly upstream and allow it to work around in the current, mending line as it swings around so as not to allow a belly to form in the fly line; this speeds the fly up and causes it to skate. The skill in fly fishing for salmon is presenting the fly so that it passes over the salmon lie as slowly as possible. In fast water this is only possible by continually mending line, and throwing a line belly upstream on the initial cast to give the fly a chance to sink.

When a salmon takes the fly it is always advisable to drop the rod tip and give the fish some line to allow it to turn before you set the hooks. If you are fishing the fly over the lie on the hover it is very important the fish has enough line to turn. This will avoid lightly lip hooking, or the fly being pushed out of its mouth most times when trying to set the hooks.

**Black Tube**
*Body*   Black floss ribbed silver tinsel
*Wing*   Black bucktail

**Black and Silver**
*Body*   Silver tinsel ribbed oval
*Wing*   Black Bucktail

**Black and Copper**
*Body*   Copper tinsel ribbed copper wire
*Wing*   Black bucktail

**Black and Orange**
*Body*   Orange wool ribbed oval gold
*Wing*   Black bucktail

**Black & Silver**
*Body*   Silver tinsel, ribbed oval
Wing   Blue and brown bucktail mixed

**Brown & Red**
*Body*   Red floss, ribbed gold oval
*Wing*   Brown bucktail

**Brown & Yellow**
*Body*   Yellow wool, ribbed gold oval
*Wing*   Brown bucktail

**Yellow & Gold**
*Body*   Gold tinsel, ribbed oval
*Wing*   Yellow bucktail

**Orange & Gold**
*Body*   Gold tinsel, ribbed oval
*Wing*   Orange bucktail

**Hot Orange**
*Body*   Orange wool, ribbed gold oval
*Wing*   Hot orange bucktail

**Red & Black**
*Body*   Black wool, ribbed silver oval
*Wing*   Red and orange bucktail mixed.

To improve the appearance of my tube flies I dress the treble hooks with a brightly dyed cock hackle which is tied in close to the hookeye and partly swept back and overtied. I consider this improves the taking qualities of the tube fly. I will leave the hackle colours to the reader; I usually match the wing colour except for the black wings then I use a red hackle for the treble hook.

**Waddington Shank Flies**
For those who require a long bodied fly without the bulk of the tube fly then the Waddington Shank is ideal. For the Waddington Shank fly and the tube fly, it is important that the hair wings are dressed long enough to mask the points of the treble hooks when they are in place.

Waddington Shanks can be purchased in all sizes ranging from 1·25 cm (¹/₂ in) right through the scale up to 6·25 cm (2¹/₂ in). One end of the shank has a loop eye which enables the knot to be used, the other end has a short loop which makes it possible to slip on the treble hook. A short length of rubber or plastic is required on the tail end of the shank to hold the treble hook in line. It pays to bind the short leg of the loop (where the treble has been placed) with silk or wire before slipping the tubing down to hold the hook in line. If at any time the treble should be damaged, the nylon and wire can be taken off which makes hook replacement very simple. The shanks can be weighted for early season when it is necessary to get the fly deep in high and cold water conditions. Tails of wool or hackles can be dressed on the treble hooks for the Waddington flies should the tyer think it is necessary.

**Black Doctor**
*Tag*   Red floss
*Body*   Black floss ribbed silver oval
*Wing*   Red bucktail with black tailover

**Blue Charm**
*Tag*   Yellow floss
*Body*   Black floss ribbed silver tinsel
*Wing*   Blue bucktail

**Ruby Moore**
*Body*   Claret floss ribbed gold oval
*Wings*   Magenta bucktail with black bucktail over

**Skunk Tail**
*Body*   Black floss ribbed silver oval
*Wing*   Blue Bucktail mixed with skunk tail

**Stewart's Killer**
*Body*   Silver tinsel ribbed oval
*Wing*   Red squirrel with black squirrel over

**Sweep**
*Body*   Black floss ribbed gold oval
*Wing*   Black squirrel
*Hackle*   Blue cock dressed as collar

**Willie Gunn**
*Body*   Black floss ribbed gold oval
*Wing*   Orange, yellow and black bucktail mixed

The tube and Waddington fly patterns listed can be interchanged thus giving a range of patterns for almost any situation and species of fish the angler is likely to meet in freshwater.

The next dressing is a realistic imitation of the elver. Elvers are young eels who run up our rivers in the spring and spend their lives in fresh water until it is time for them to make the return trip as fully grown adults to their spawning grounds in the sea.

This pattern is dressed using the tail and body of a Delta plastic eel whipped on a longshank hook, with a longfibre blue hackle tied in close to the hookeye, swept back and overtied, thus veiling the body.

### Elver fly
*Body and Tail*   Grey or blue Delta plastic eel
*Hackle*   Long fibre blue cock
*Hook*   Longshank size 1/0

A very useful addition to the angler's fly box, it is effective throughout the season.

Ragot of Loudeac supply a useful range of poppers which are of American origin. These poppers have solid bell shape cork heads with a flat front. The bulk of the cork head is above the hookshank followed by a hackle and two hackles forming the tails. The cork head is secured to the hookshank by cutting a narrow slot in the cork, pressing the hookshank into the slot and gluing. If the depth of the slot is kept shallow the bulk of the cork bell will be above the hookshank.

### Minnow Popper
*Tail*   Two cree hackles
*Hackle*   Cree cock
*Head*   Cork bell shaped painted green with white eye

### Froggie Popper
*Tail*   Two cree hackles dyed yellow
*Hackle*   Cree cock
*Head*   Cork painted dark green with rubber legs in front and rear

### Dixie Devil
*Tail*   Two white cock hackles
*Hackle*   Black cork
*Head*   Cork painted white with white rubber legs in front and rear

### Bee Bug Popper
*Tail*   Two brown partridge hackles dressed flat
*Head*   Cork painted black with yellow stripes, white rubber legs in front and rear

### Dynamite
*Tail*   Dyed yellow cock
*Hackle*   Black cock
*Head*   Cork painted brown with white rubber legs in front and rear

### Sneaky Pete
*Tail*   Dyed orange cock
*Hackle*   Black cock
*Head*   Cork painted orange

### Bass King Popper
*Tail*   Dyed yellow cock hackles
*Hackle*   Black cock
*Head*   Cork painted bright yellow, rubber legs front and rear

### Bass Duster Popper
*Tail*   Dyed yellow cock hackles
*Hackle*   Black cock
*Head*   Cork painted green with white rubber legs front and rear

Weighted flies have become popular in recent years. The following flies have the advantages of the improved hooking capacity of the flying X 2B Partridge treble and of being heavily weighted. Their construction consists of a size 14 treble hook on a nylon trace which is joined to a size 6 wide gape hook. The nylon brace between the two hooks should be approx. 4 cm (1½ in) long.

The dressing of these flies is very simple, assuming the flying treble and front hook trace is already completed. Place the front hook in the vice and wind a strip of lead wire from hookeye to bend. Now whip on the silk thus securing the lead. Tie a tail of marabou fibres mixed with crystal hair about 5 cm (2 in) long encircling the hookshank, thereby veiling the flying treble hook. Tie in wool and ribbing, wind the wool to form the body and secure; tie in the hackle and wind palmer style down the hookshank, then wind the ribbing up the hookshank, securing the hackle. Cut off surplus ribbing, whip finish and varnish. The leaded body of the front hook of this design makes it a heavier lure than the normal lead head designs and with the sting in the tail of the flying X2B Partridge treble it makes a very effective design, with superior hooking capabilities when compared to standard longshank leadhead designs.

**Orange Stinger**
*Hook*   Wide gape size six with size 14 treble in tandem
*Tail*   Orange marabou mixed silver crystal hair
*Body*   Orange wool ribbed gold wire
*Hackle*   Furnace cock palmer style

**Black Stinger**
*Hook*   Wide gape size 6 with size 14 treble in tandem
*Tail*   Black marabou mixed silver crystal hair
*Body*   Black wool ribbed silver wire
*Hackle*   Black cock palmer style

**Yellow Stinger**
*Hook*   Wide gape size 6 with size 14 treble in tandem
*Tail*   Yellow marabou mixed silver crystal hair
*Body*   Yellow wool ribbed copper wire
*Hackle*   Cree cock palmer style

**White Stinger**
*Hook*   Wide gape size 6 with size 14 treble in tandem
*Tail*   White marabou mixed silver crystal hair
*Body*   Red wool ribbed silver wire
*Hackle*   Badger cock palmer style.

The above patterns have proved very effective over a wide range of fishing waters and conditions, particularly when fished in fast running water on short leaders for sea trout.

The hook sizes are the tyer's choice. It is important however that the marabou tail is dressed on the front hook so that it encircles the hookshank thus veiling the flying treble hook.